Gavin Bolton
essential writings

Gavin Bolton
essential writings

edited by David Davis

Trentham Books

Stoke on Trent, UK and Sterling, USA

Winner of the IPG DIVERSITY Award 2010

Trentham Books Limited
Westview House   22883 Quicksilver Drive
734 London Road   Sterling
Oakhill   VA 20166-2012
Stoke on Trent   USA
Staffordshire
England ST4 5NP

First published 2010

British Library Cataloguing-in-Publication Data
A catalogue record for this book is available from the British Library

ISBN: 978 1 85856 470 8

Designed and typeset by Trentham Books Ltd and printed in
Great Britain by CMP (UK) Ltd, Dorset

We are grateful to the following for permission to reproduce copyright material by Gavin Bolton:

Simon and Schuster for parts of Chapter 4 'Teacher as fellow artist' part of Chapter 6 'Aims and objectives' and Chapter 7 'Assessment' from *New perspectives in classroom drama*; Pearson Education for part of Chapter 6 on 'Protection into role' from *Drama as Education* and 'Drama and Meaning', 'Drama in education – a re-appraisal', 'An Evaluation of the Schools Council Drama Teaching Project' and 'Drama in education: learning medium or arts process?' from *Selected Writings*; National Association for the Teaching of Drama for 'Piss on his face', 'Education and dramatic art: a personal review' and 'Although'; National Drama for 'It's all theatre' and 'Have a heart' and, of course, Trentham Books for the extracts from *Acting in classroom drama*.

Contents

For Gavin
And my two Elaines

Acknowledgements

First and foremost I want to thank Gavin for a professional lifetime's support and friendship. A leader in the field of drama, he is one of the few people I have met who, having gained a world-wide reputation, has remained self-effacing, non-defensive and open to criticism, his own as well as that of others. As well as his remarkable clarity of thinking, I have never known him manipulate others for his own advantage. I have always found him to be totally honest with himself and others and able to weave a course through other people's ideas without making an enemy of them. I realise this is reading like a reference and I make no apology for that. I want to mark Gavin Bolton out for the extraordinary individual he is: a vanishing breed in this world of greater and greater cutthroat competition. My thanks to him also for answering many questions while preparing this selection and for reading and commenting on the Introduction and for having the last word in this volume.

This collection would not have been prepared in time without the invaluable editing of scanned material by my wife Elaine. I owe her more than I can repay her for time given generously and for the calm, sheer goodness she brings to my life.

My thanks to Chris Cooper, Bill Roper and Kate Katafiasz for many years of friendship and intellectual stimulation in the fields of drama, philosophy and aesthetics. And to Mike Fleming, for more than forty years of trusted and respected colleagueship.

Thanks to Cecily for many years of professional generosity and stimulating writing and teaching and for writing the Foreword.

Finally, many thanks to Gillian Klein, Trentham's editor for the Drama Series, for her clear advice and support. She is at the helm of a remarkable educational publishing house where principles predominate over profit, almost impossible to find in such abundance elsewhere in the publishing world.

Foreword

This important collection will remind those who already know Bolton's work of his profound significance in the development of drama in education. New readers will be will be challenged, provoked and inspired by the range of his thinking.

Gavin Bolton was a scholar and university teacher of immense generosity and openness. I had the advantage of being a student on his MA course at the University of Durham in the 1970s. He shared his thinking with his students as he was putting the finishing touches to *Towards a Theory of Drama in Education* (Bolton, 1979) and taught us the core principles of scholarship – to recognise and respect the work of those who had gone before us in the field and to acknowledge our sources. As he developed his theories in later books, he was always prepared to revisit his ideas in the light of fresh insights of his own or from other theorists, and to subject them to close scrutiny and if necessary, revision. Bolton had an unparalleled ability to analyse and critique his own theory and practice with humour and honesty.

Although he is probably best known as a theorist, all of his thinking is firmly based on his practical experience. As a practitioner, Bolton's calm manner made it easy for students of all ages to trust him and become engaged in the work. His skill in finding the appropriate way to distance the drama provided a safe point of engagement for participants. Bolton always acknowledged Dorothy Heathcote as the major source of his inspiration but where her practice often left observers paralysed in awe at her gifts as an educator, Bolton's demeanour gave lesser teachers the confidence that they too might one day achieve similar outcomes. His energy in the classroom was always under control and his skill in finding a focus for the drama was remarkable. Those who have seen him work will remember the sensitivity and flexibility with which he responded to any unexpected or inappropriate contributions.

An expert in any field has been defined as someone who knows how to deal with the unexpected. The difficulty about observing experts is that although the results of their work may be evident, the means by which they achieve those results is often invisible. Some observers find Heathcote's teaching astonishing but impenetrable. Bolton and Heathcote both drew participants into an immediate, unpremeditated and intense participation in moments of lived experience. But Bolton also possessed the ability to articulate his thought processes with great clarity, as he negotiated the unpredictable possibilities in what he used to call 'living-through' drama.

The environment in which I first encountered Bolton's work was profoundly different to that which exists today. Drama lessons mostly consisted of games and improvisation exercises, and small group play-making was popular. Like other drama teachers at the time, personal growth and creativity were the objectives of my lessons. Although these sessions may have exhibited a great deal of energy from both teacher and students, there was no coherent context and very little significant content. However creative and enjoyable they may have been for the participants, such sequences of disconnected activities were unlikely to deliver any depth of learning or insight, or indeed any aesthetic outcomes. Growth and learning in any discipline will always depend on a sequence of related activities rather than single, unconnected ones.

During a weekend workshop led by Bolton in the 70s, I realised for the first time that it was possible for every strategy, game or exercise included in the session to illuminate and deepen the drama context. A drama lesson could incorporate each of the categories that Bolton had identified – exercise, living through and theatre form – but these would be selected to serve the developing dramatic situation.

The novelist Henry James was spectacularly unsuccessful in his attempts to write plays, but he understood the significance of dramatic episodes as well as the most effective playwright. In his introduction to *The Awkward Age*, he writes that he wanted every scene in the novel to be like a lamp illuminating a single occasion in the lives of the characters, and revealing the relevance of that occasion for the theme of the book. Ideally, in structuring what has come to be known as Process Drama, each strategy, scene or episode should operate in a similar fashion. The work progresses though a sequence of related episodes, each one shining a different light on the emerging drama.

Bolton had a deep understanding of the fundamental nature of theatre and knew that drama worked best when it operated according to the rules of theatre. In *Drama as Education* (Bolton, 1984) he stresses that it is the 'inner dynamic' of the situation, that moves the drama forward rather than the sequential actions of 'what happens next'. This understanding has eluded many drama practitioners. Lord Byron, for example, objected to Shakespeare's lack of originality in terms of plot and claimed that he had no invention as to stories but merely threw the stories of others into dramatic shape.

To give *dramatic shape* to old stories – Byron makes light of this talent, but it is the key attribute of the dramatist. If we work in devised theatre or process drama our task is the same one. Of all that I learned from Bolton, perhaps the most important was the realisation that the structure of process drama – 'the mutual relationship between elements of the dramatic event' (Bolton, 1984:90) – will resonate with theatre form. It has always mystified me that Bolton's work has been seen as being in opposition to theatre. Any intelligent reading of his books or observation of his practice quickly dispels this inaccurate impression.

Bolton knew that it is a mistake to believe that students have had an aesthetic education just because they have acquired a great deal of conceptual knowledge about theatre and drama. It is very easy, especially in light of the current focus on skills and instrumental learning, for teachers to move imperceptibly from an open, intuitive approach to a mechanistic one, with an emphasis on de-contextualised skills and inactive knowledge. For Bolton, learning *about* theatre should never replace learning *in* and *through* theatre.

This collection makes it very clear why Gavin Bolton's theory and practice has had such a profound and positive effect on the landscape of drama in education. I am proud to claim him as my teacher, my mentor and my friend.

Cecily O'Neill

Introduction

All Gavin Bolton's books about his own work are now out of print. I notice that *Acting in Classroom Drama* (1998), perhaps his most important book, is for sale on Amazon on the day I write this, for over £218! Some people must still be very keen to get hold of his writings.

Gavin Bolton has been a leading figure in drama in education for over 50 years. His name has been linked with Dorothy Heathcote for the major part of that time. It seems as though it has always been 'Heathcote and Bolton' when referring to the leading international figures in drama teaching. However, he has graciously acknowledged her as the leading figure and a genius in the field. Dorothy Heathcote made nearly all the major innovations in classroom drama teaching and continues to do so on into her 80s. While Heathcote invented new drama forms and teaching methods it was Bolton who became the major writer to try to pin down his and Heathcote's practice in a theoretical form accessible internationally. After Heathcote developed Mantle of the Expert, Bolton, while recognising the great importance of this approach to education, did not pursue it himself and went on to make his own way in the field of drama teaching. In four major books developing his own approach to the theory and practice of drama in education, in another three books written with and about Heathcote's work and in over 70 articles and chapters for journals and books, Gavin Bolton has probably been the most prolific writer internationally, and certainly the leading writer internationally, in this field. In his own right he has taught and influenced thousands of teachers in his postgraduate courses, summer schools all over the world, in-service courses for education authorities and for drama associations, national and international.

Two little known areas of his expertise were voluntary work with mental health patients in a local psychiatric hospital once a week during term time and after he retired, voluntary work for Victim Support using role-play, particularly with young children traumatised, for example, by having found a burglar in the house.

I have known Gavin Bolton since 1969, when I studied with him on his Postgraduate Diploma course, and have valued his friendship for over 40 years. I suspect we are both a little surprised to find ourselves in our 70s and 80s respectively. The only time I can remember getting cross with him was preparing for this present volume, when I found out that he destroyed his archive of work after he knew that he had finally finished teaching! Not even a recent list of *all* his writings is available. This has made assembling the present collection difficult. I have collected a list of as many of his writings as I can find which can be found at the end of this volume.

I have chosen to focus on those of his writings that developed his latest thinking about classroom drama, those that cover major areas of his interests and also those where he has taken up the defence of drama in education against those who have sought to undermine it, if not destroy it. For every piece of writing that I have included, I have had to reject three that were vying for importance. In fact, his writing can almost be sorted into three major fields: the development of his own approach to drama teaching; his own original contributions to theory and practice; and where he has felt impelled to defend drama teaching from destructive attacks. This latter area has often also served as the means to refine and develop his own theoretical understanding.

I cannot claim that these are **the** essential writings but just that they are **some** of the essential writings. To have chosen what I consider to be the definitive list would have meant at least three volumes of writings which was economically impracticable. Instead, I have chosen what represent some of his key writings. Another, editor would have most likely made different choices.

Before beginning to elaborate on these areas, I want to draw attention to one central quality Bolton has maintained all his working life: his great humility. Hopefully, there will be readers who were still at school when Bolton finished running courses and have never had the privilege of meeting him. These are the readers he addresses primarily in his Afterword. Only too often one comes across people who have made a name for themselves in a field and the main interest of these people is in themselves and in their own self-promotion. Bolton is the opposite. An example of his humility, misplaced on this occasion, was in thinking that no one would be interested in his writings and his archive. Early on, in his first book he wrote:

> I have made, and still make, many mistakes when working with children, but I happen to be blessed with those two contradictory qualities essential perhaps for all drama teachers – a humility to recognise my mistakes combined with an arrogance of certainty that I can not only learn from them but also abstract a sufficiently firm philosophy from the experience to write a book about it! (Bolton, 1979:2)

One of the ways I was tempted to approach selecting from his writings was to show those which developed and refined his thinking over time. However, there was not space to do this. Instead, I have chosen to present those texts that capture his latest thinking up to and beyond his retirement and simply to draw attention, in this introduction, to how his thinking developed over time.

What was fundamental to his approach to drama teaching? I think he captured it pretty well in 1971 when he asked and began to answer the key questions he has pursued ever since.

> What is drama? When is drama, drama? When does educational drama go to the heart of drama? We should be able to ask this question: what is the nature and function of drama when it operates at its highest level of achievement?
>
> It seems to me that possibly an answer to this is, when it is composed of those elements that are common to both children's play and to theatre, when the aims are to help children to learn about those feelings, attitudes and preconceptions that, before the drama was experienced, were too implicit for them to be aware of. [...so they are] helped to face facts and to interpret them without prejudice; so that they develop a range and degree of identification with other people; so that they develop a set of principles, a set of consistent principles, by which they are going to live. (Bolton, 1971:12-13)

This could serve as a basic template for his life-long concerns: the relationship of drama to play; the cognitive/affective nature of the experience; the relationship of children's play, dramatic playing and theatre; and helping children to understand the social world around them and their relationship to it.

Building on the above, his first book, *Towards a theory of drama in education,* develops the above concerns and sets out pretty well all the main areas that he pursued from the 1970s onwards. First and foremost he wants drama to challenge: '...the major problem in drama in this country is not that basic values are being challenged, but that nothing is being challenged at all.' (Bolton, 1979:135) This raises the questions: What sort of drama will do this? What are the modes of involvement that will engage young people most productively in this process?

He is one of the few leaders in the field who have built their approach on the direct relationship of child drama to children's make-believe play. Other notable figures to do this are Peter Slade (1954) and Richard Courtney (1968). In fact, for a long time he termed the most important mode of involvement in drama 'dramatic playing'. Later he came to prefer 'living through drama' which sprang into being whenever a teacher in role was employed and finally he uses the term 'making' drama for this special mode of involvement (Bolton, 1998). He built on the fundamental notion that play uses 'being' to 'explore being'. The children are able to be themselves and other people and somewhere else at the same time. He came to use the term *metaxis*, which he borrowed from Boal, to describe this dialectic. It is this mode of engagement with role, being in the event while able to monitor and reflect on it at the same time with the power of theatre form, that he has sought to refine throughout his teaching, using this engagement to confront the children with themselves in relation to the social world of which they are an intrinsic part.

In this first book, he goes on to elaborate other areas that would continue to intrigue him. He moved from an early interest in Piaget to Bruner and Vygotsky as the more useful educational psychologists. He had come across Vygotsky's important article on child play (Vygotsky, 1933) and from Vygotsky he saw the fundamental importance of working in the Zone of Proximal Development: working ahead of the child's actual ability so that learning precedes and influences development. Not, as in Piaget, presuming that development precedes and dictates the learning level. This led him to see that the teacher had to structure the drama learning experience so that it provided a scaffold for the child's learning and subsequent development.

He became intrigued by the way the art form of drama could be integrated with dramatic playing. He began the elaboration of exactly how the art form of theatre is fundamental to dramatic playing. He picked out *tension* with sub-sections dealing with the special *sense of time* in drama, focus dealing with the tension in the material itself and the tension that comes through *surprise*. He also took as major components of the art form *contrast* in its various forms and *symbolisation*, using objects and actions to go beyond the literal to hold layers of focused meanings. Symbolisation he considered then and later to be 'the most important part of this book' (Bolton, 1979:83). Paradoxically, he argued for drama as *not* doing but as essentially a mental activity, 'thought in action', although the mental activity was focused through dramatic action.

He was the first to see the importance of secondary symbolism or, at least, the first to write about it and name it in relation to drama. Drawing on Piaget (1972) he uses the example of a child who, in play, may use a doll to represent a person, the primary level of symbolism, but also, subconsciously, to represent his or her annoying new baby brother who needs to be sent on a long journey. This became a crucial element of his drama as he tried to read the other, hidden levels of significance in the roles his pupils chose to play.

Bolton, to the best of my knowledge, was also the first to elaborate the notion of the second dimension of role. He used this term to describe the useful technique of helping the class find a way into their role by seeking out a collective relationship to the role. This relationship needed to connect with what they already knew as young people of a particular age in a particular culture to the collective role they were bringing to life. So if they were to be pirates, a way in might be through a second dimension of role as novice pirates or home-sick pirates or pirates having to conceal their identity in order to buy provisions in town. This second dimension found a connection between the child's life and the life of the role; it found a way of connecting the young people with each other in role; and found a way of connecting them all in role with the central theme of the drama. This was first elaborated in a paper only published in *Gavin Bolton: selected writings* (Bolton, 1972) and is developed in *Towards a theory of drama in education* (1979:61-62).

Also in his first book we find the important notion of the angle of connection between the pupil in role and the material being worked on (Bolton, 1979:60). This is an area that the drama teacher ignores at his or her peril. Without it the pupils may have no real engagement with or excitement in the material. An excellent example of the teacher working to find this angle of connection appears in *Towards a theory of drama in education* (1979). The pupils had chosen to do a play about the conflict in Northern Ireland that was raging at the time. The boys immediately divided themselves into IRA members and Provisionals. The girls said they did not want to take sides. They said they wanted to keep out of the 'troubles'. Bolton found both the angle of connection and a second dimension of role by setting the conflict in and outside a supermarket. The girls could start by shopping, carrying on as normal, life must go on, and the boys could be eyeing each other up for potential trouble outside. After the conflict ensued and the police officer arrived (teacher in role) to find the men gone, he arrested all the women to take them away for questioning, no matter how much they protested that they were not involved and had not seen what happened. This is a neat example of teacher helping to structure the play the class wanted to do, to help them find a way in and then use surprise to shift the focus of the drama. 'The women were whisked off for questioning by this 'brutal' police officer [...and] under this kind of pressure, were resentful, angry, upset and astonished. Something of the misery and hopelessness of the Irish situation dawned on them' (Bolton, 1979:80-81).

Bolton took over Geoff Gillham's notion of there being two plays functioning at the same time: the 'play for class' and 'the play for teacher'. The children's angle of connection is the 'play for them'. The play for teacher involves weaving in the components of the art form: the structure that will enable the engagement with significant learning areas for the pupils, as in the example above. This is probably the most referred to unpublished paper in the history of drama in education (Gillham, 1974).

He also developed the important notion of 'constraints' to describe the crucial dimension of the art form which delays the moment of conflict to produce tension: the immanence of conflict. (See the extract on this topic in this volume).

All these areas are fundamental to Bolton's life-long concerns: a search for the most useful mode of engagement with role, involving exploring the relationship of make believe play to dramatic playing; the structure that would enable a felt change of appraisal; the unity of reason and feeling, 'affective cognitive development' (Bolton, 1979:39) to achieve a 'personal shift in value' (*Ibid*: 90); the search for theatre form in classroom drama; the responsibility of the teacher to help with this process leading towards the autonomous control of the art form at a later stage. All these areas mark him out as a teacher, embedded in practice, and not a theoretician. All his writings about this practice spring from his own teaching. He is not a theoretician, walled off from the classroom like some of his critics.

In the 1970s and 80s these critical voices started to be raised. Witkin (1974) argued that educational drama had not found the ability to use the art form. Malcolm Ross at Exeter University accused Bolton and Heathcote of being anti-theatre and highly manipulative teachers, interfering with children's creativity (see Ross, 1982). David Hornbrook, a lecturer at a college of further education, began to open broadsides against both Bolton and Heathcote, with similar accusations, that they were destroying the art of theatre in schools. He described their work as devoid of social content without offering any moral compass. In *Education and Dramatic Art* he wrote:

> Without doubt this is the vacuum at the centre of drama-in-education, the existential, narcissistic wilderness around which students circle in search of truth, value and meaning, but in which all the so-called social learning of the drama class, however conscientiously engineered, must in the end be condemned to wander aimlessly. (Hornbook, 1998:68)

How Hornbook can claim this in the light of many similar examples to the one above, about living in Northern Ireland, makes one wonder if he and other critics really knew anything about what actually happened in drama lessons. In the same volume he likened Heathcote and Bolton to Muggletonians. Reeve and his cousin Muggleton led a radical puritan sect in 17th century England. People who came to them could have the true word of God revealed to them.

> [drama teachers] could forsake the discourse of the wider educational community in favour of the witness of 'Dorothy and Gavin'. For, like Reeve and Muggleton, Heathcote and Bolton offered a wisdom that claimed its origins in a deep spiritual truth and a unifying vision of humanity which absolved their follower from further moral or ideological speculation. (*Ibid*:26)

Hornbook called his second book *Education in drama*, turning drama in education on its head to highlight his view that drama was a subject, and that subject was theatre arts.

Peter Abbs, at the University of Sussex, wrote open letters to Bolton. These are reproduced in one of Abbs' books under the chapter heading of 'Educational drama as cultural dispossession'. The chapter consists of three documents in which he makes the case that 'educational drama over the last three or four decades has badly neglected the aesthetic field of drama, namely the continuum of theatre' (Abbs, 1994: 117-8).

It is hard now to remember the ferocity of the battles that raged in the 80s and early 90s. In fact, Bolton and Heathcote have always seen themselves as using the same clay, employing the same components of the art form that have developed in theatre. Heathcote's response was mainly to ignore the challenge and just get on with her teaching regarding this as the best reply. She wrote a letter to Hornbrook saying how amused she had been by the Muggletonians reference. Bolton, on the other hand, took up the cudgels on behalf of classroom drama teachers who were having to argue for the validity of their subject to school heads and parents. (See examples of this defence in the latter part of this volume.)

This rift in the educational drama community had its origins in the hostility to theatre in schools argued for by Peter Slade and Brian Way, early pioneers of classroom drama. In the 70s the desire to find a place for classroom drama in the curriculum tended to hide the fact that it was intrinsically using theatre form in the process. By the mid-90s these disagreements had largely been overcome by those, including Bolton, who were able to show that classroom drama and theatre used the same art form, and that what was needed was an integrated approach (see Fleming, 2001). Indeed one of Bolton's latest writings on the subject was called 'It's all theatre' (see this volume).

Bolton, in all the books about his own work, has sought to overcome these divisions and to defend and develop the use of classroom drama, often with humour (see *Piss on his face*), with erudition (see *Drama in education: learning medium or arts process*), and only once with sarcasm and hardly concealed anger, drawn to my attention by Mike Fleming, *Have a heart* (all these in this volume). The latter is difficult to justify as an 'essential' writing, but I have selected it as an example of the passion with which he has defended the uniqueness of 'making' drama as a form of dramatic art.

In his second book, *Drama as education* (Bolton, 1984), referring to these divisions in drama teaching, he writes 'I wish to rectify the balance by taking a broader view and by introducing a theoretical framework through which an eclectic view might be sustained' (p1). His following book (*New perspectives on classroom drama*, 1992) was an implicit reply to the critique of David Hornbrook and others, setting out his theory and practice in detail. The book after this, *Acting in classroom drama* (Bolton,

1998), was a direct response to Hornbrook who had written: 'It is my contention that conceptually there is nothing which differentiates the child acting in the classroom from the actor on the stage of the theatre' (cited in Bolton, 1998:xvi). In fact, having retired, at this stage in his life, he at last had time to do a PhD and he wrote some 180,000 words on just this one sentence: a model I hold up for my own PhD students of how to keep a tight focus! The book is adapted from the thesis and in 284 pages he builds his argument to prove Hornbrook wrong.

In the 20 years spanned by these four books, Bolton has modified and developed his basic understanding of the modes of involvement possible and preferable in classroom drama and the sort of learning which is desirable. To start with, in *Towards a theory of drama in education* (1979), he saw four separately identifiable but interconnected modes: dramatic playing, exercise and theatre, and Type D, which combined the other three. The learning was much more conceptually based. The learning area could be described in propositional terms. In *Drama as education* the modes of involvement are on a continuum, on a sliding dialectic between an intention to be and an intention to describe (p125). The pupils have no focal awareness of the learning area and what is being learned cannot be put into propositional terms (p153). By the time he writes *Acting in classroom drama* (1998) he makes a clear distinction between three modes of involvement: making, presenting and performing. Making is now qualitatively different from the other two and is what makes classroom drama unique. His other major development from *New perspectives* onwards is to adopt an ethnomethodological approach to role building. 'The participants in 'living through' drama behave as we all behave when we make an effort to present a social event to each other in 'real life" (Bolton, 1998:181) The participants work at making the social event until, along with the focusing 'distortions' of the art form, 'I am making it happen' becomes 'It is happening to me and I am able to be aware of what is happening to me.' It is a social negotiation of meanings. This final theoretical underpinning builds on the early influence of Hall's (1959) *The silent language*. Hall was an important early influence on both Heathcote and Bolton, a text which elaborates how all of us can only be human through a particular culture with any strengths and weaknesses that may be embedded in the social history of that culture. Role building must therefore involve working at and recognising those 'hidden' rules that govern our interactions.

Forced to limit my selection of writings, I have started with key later writings which set out some of his most developed thinking. This makes for a slightly concentrated start to the book but it means that Bolton's latest thinking about classroom drama is available at the outset. Starting with an example of Bolton's skilled classroom drama practice at its best, I have then retained the lengthy description of Peter Millward's work with a group of young children as, an understanding of this section and its importance to Bolton, is key to understanding the essence of his approach. After these, I have tried to pick out writings which capture key contributions he has made to drama teaching theory. In the final section I have made a selection of extracts defending drama in education from the attacks mentioned above, as well as a response to an important publication: the National Curriculum Council's *Arts in Schools* Report.

I finish the selection with Bolton's final attempt to bridge the drama/theatre divide, a pursuit he has made all his professional life, with *It's all theatre*. Rather than give an introduction here to each of the items in the book, I have described them briefly in the text. Where it is an extract from a book, I have left in original references to other sections of the same book. Where Harvard referencing has been used I have retained this and placed all the references at the end of the book. In some places, I have edited the text by reducing the length where this has not interfered with the meaning. I have indicated where all these take place.

References

Bolton, G (1971) Drama and theatre in education: a survey In *Drama and theatre in education* Dodd, N and Hickson, W (Eds) London:Heinemann

Bolton, G (1972) Further notes for Bristol teachers on the 'second dimension' In *Gavin Bolton: selected writings* (1986) London and New York: Longman

Bolton, G (1979) *Towards a theory of drama in education* London: Longman

Bolton, G (1984) *Drama as education* Longman

Bolton, G (1992) *New perspectives on classroom drama* Simon and Schuster Education

Bolton, G (1998) *Acting in classroom drama: a critical analysis* Trentham Books

Bolton, G (2010) Personal email

Courtney, R (1968) *Play, drama and thought* Simon and Pierre

Fleming, M (2001) *Teaching drama in primary and secondary schools: an integrated approach* David Fulton Publishers

Gillham, G (1974) Condercum school report for Newcastle upon Tyne LEA (unpublished)

Hall, Edward T (1959) *The Silent Language* Doubleday, Chicago

Hornbrook, D (1998) *Education and Dramatic Art* (2nd Ed.)

Piaget, J (1972) *Play, dreams and imitation in childhood* London: Routledge and Kegan Paul

Ross, M (1982) *The development of aesthetic experience* Curriculum series in the arts Vol 3, Pergammon Press

Slade, P (1954) *Child drama* University of London Press

Vygotsky, L (1933) Play and its role in the mental development of the child. In Bruner, J S et al (1976) *Play: its development and evolution* Penguin

Witkin, R W (1974) *The intelligence of feeling* London: Heinemann Educational books

KEY WRITINGS ON THE NATURE OF CLASSROOM DRAMA

Re-interpretations of Dorothy Heathcote's 'living through' drama

Edited extracts from Chapter 10 of *Acting in classroom drama:
a critical analysis* (1998)

This was Bolton's final book about his own work and, in many ways, the most important. He wrote it in response to David Hornbrook's claim that acting in the theatre was exactly the same as in classroom drama. In this book Bolton traces key developments and forms of classroom drama in the UK from the Victorian period to the present day. He provides an analysis of these developments, coming to the conclusion that Hornbrook is mistaken and that *Making* in classroom drama is a qualitatively different mode of involvement from acting in the theatre. He elaborates and justifies this in Chapter 11 of the same book which follows this one in its entirety and in the extract I have chosen from Chapter 10, he describes a key example of his own approach to classroom drama and a key source and influence on his adoption of an ethnomethodological stance to best describe his approach to role building and meaning making. I have included the lengthy description of Millward's teaching as Bolton's obvious regard for it indicates that this as a key example of the way that dramatic playing develops into a unique form of drama and how they link together: an example that he builds on in the following chapter. Both these extracts are best read together. I have omitted in these two extracts the many useful notes that accompanied the original as a space-saving measure but have gathered, at the end of the book, the references to texts mentioned.

The first section of this chapter will present a more personal account of my own work than I intended to include. It was never within my plan to cast myself as a pioneer in drama education, on the grounds that whereas I may have made some original theoretical contribution to the field I have always felt that my work was largely derivative, indebted as I am to Peter Slade, Brian Way, Dorothy Heathcote and to others in amateur and professional theatre, but it has become pressingly obvious now to me that I have to a large extent been responsible for a reinterpretation of Heathcote's methodology that has taken 'living through' Drama in a direction never intended by her and perhaps, from her point of view, off-target, if not misguided.

A new direction for 'living through'

The point has already been made in the previous chapter that emotional engagement and detachment characterised all Heathcote's work. The evident modification of emotional engagement did not always protect her from misinterpretation – by her followers as well as her critics. That emotions could arise naturally and sometimes powerfully from an agreed make-believe context appealed to the imaginations of some of her admirers who saw new possibilities in drama workshops. Just as leading directors in theatre were beginning to experiment in rehearsals with somatic means of generating feeling, some leaders in the classroom were setting up intensely emotional dramatic contexts. 'Living through' became associated with 'deep' emotional experiences.

Imperceptibly, in the hands of some of Heathcote's emulators (I include myself here), the target group for 'living through' drama changed from Heathcote's 'pupil-centred' work to 'adult-centred' (usually teachers) refreshment. In-service training was in vogue and almost every local education authority in this country committed itself to running week-end drama courses for its teachers.

My own contribution to such courses set a pattern of almost total workshop participation. Thus 'living through' drama became accepted by some as something *adults* successfully did together and there is little doubt that these groups of highly committed teachers gradually transformed the potential of this way of dramatising. It became a carefully crafted and deeply felt theatre experience – important in itself and only incidentally committed to learning something. Typically, as 'the experience' came to a close, the questions immediately pursued would relate to 'how was it for you?' and/or 'how did you feel?', *questions Dorothy Heathcote would never find herself asking.* Only after this personal debriefing would the week-end course or the Summer School get round to asking: 'How might we apply this experience to the pupils we teach?', an example, to Dorothy Heathcote, of 'putting the cart before the horse', although she 'has no quarrel' in principle with the idea of adults 'exploring what it's like to participate in drama work'.

One of the dangers of this 'experiential' approach was that some who had found the kind of workshops described above as personally satisfying, mistakenly associated the new genre with therapy, a view far from my own and sickeningly offensive to Dorothy Heathcote. There is little doubt that all the arts and any other satisfying experience (like, for some, 'gardening') may be therapeutic, but that cannot be and must not be a goal in an educational setting. Another danger in this approach was that its exponents, at least in the 1970s, zealously confined the dramatic form to an improvisational mode, eschewing alternative forms such as script, exercises and depiction. Preliminary tasks might be necessary to set up the theme, but, once launched, it was thought that sustained, whole class improvisation offered the most potent experience. Its 'success' often depended on the intensity of the theme, providing a dynamic sustainable through a whole workshop. Given skilled leadership and commitment by the participants this sustained approach often worked, participants claiming they had had a worthwhile experience. In our enthusiasm for engaging with significant themes, we failed to notice that Dorothy Heathcote was gradually turning away from drama as 'A Man in a Mess'.

A word should be said here about the BBC films that have given Dorothy Heathcote's work such prominence. Because the cameras did their work well the acting behaviour of individual children in the 'Stool Pigeon' and 'Death of a President', scenes may have become inflated in the minds of spectators. When, for instance the 'Stool Pigeon' breaks down and weeps, this appears to be a remarkable moment of natural, spontaneous expression of emotion (some might be led to think, epitomising Heathcote's work at its best). It was, however, a piece of effective contrivance between an astute film director and the boy actor who had previously raised the question with Heathcote and the class whether it would appropriate for his character to cry. Likewise the deft hiding of the keys when the guards suddenly arrive, had been worked out technically ready for the camera to 'make authentic'. More importantly from Heathcote's point of view, much of the preparation for the scene was taken up with building 'self-spectatorship' in all the boys and a rational examination of how people like guards signal power. By the time they 'performed' for the cameras, their engagement was as much an intellectual understanding as a 'feeling' experience. Reading Davis' 'What is 'depth' in educational drama?' (Davis, 1976) one is left with the impression that he, like many of us, saw it as a camera fortuitously picking up on a child's moment of shock at having betrayed his friends. Of course, in some sense, this was the case, but Heathcote knows the emotion of the incident was properly backed with intelligent calculation, understanding and self-awareness.

An example of my own teaching

I have elected to describe below a sequence from my own teaching that I believe typifies the attempt to discover an elaborate, sophisticated sequence of dramatic experiences (using a variety of dramatic forms, but having, at some point, a 'significant' existential, 'living through', element) that aimed to build some kind of satisfying theatrical experience.

A lesson devised originally for adolescents preparing to study 'The Crucible' by Arthur Miller

This is an elaborate form of 'living though' drama, a dramatic sequence sustaining a single thematic cycle of experience, depending, as we shall see, on many dramatic forms. A version of the plan was first used with adolescents in the late 1980s, and later in adult workshops. The description below was written as part of a 'teaching' document for students of drama education.

One of the difficulties for young pupils engaging with a dramatic text based on historical material is that their grasp on the hidden values of a 'strange' culture such as Puritan Massachusetts in the 17th century is too slender for them to make connections with their own lives. They may be inclined to regard people who were prepared to burn witches as quaint or mad or too childish to be worth bothering with. My purpose therefore in setting up a drama experience about the play before they read the script was to whet their appetites and to make the circumstances of the play seem more familiar.

In Miller's text he introduces the idea (based on historical fact) that a group of young girls gained so much power over the community that by merely pointing an accusing finger at any adult in the community, that victim would be sent to the stake.

My initial task towards preparing this lesson was to find a *pivotal* scene which would portray the period while at the same time capturing the sense of potential power over parents lying within the hands of their off-spring (I did not make a distinction, as Miller did, between boys and girls). The picture in my head, drawn from Miller's play, was of a community of families torn by rumour that some of their adolescent children might have been dancing naked in the nearby woods and engaging in black magic. I knew that, unless the class I was going to work with were very experienced, a confrontation between parents and children or any attempt at giving them the experience of 'dancing in the woods' would deteriorate into embarrassed flippancy or empty technique, for they would simply be engaged in presenting the surface of incidents rather than grappling with the implicit values underlying the incidents.

This is undoubtedly the drama teacher's continual dilemma – how may a class of pupils begin to engage with a culture's deepest values before they have any real grasp of either those values or the contexts in which those values might be expressed? In the early days of drama teaching, we used to rely on 'characterisation' as providing a base from which to begin, which we now realise is a dramatic *cul de sac*, for it too hastily sketches psychological differences at the expense of cultural sharing. It is of little educational and dramatic use to give the young actors a chance to enjoy defying their 'parents' if they have no shared understanding of a cultural system that is based on respect – for parents and the authority of the church and fear of God. To engage in an act of deceiving and lying to 'parents', however lively the improvisation may seem, actually takes the pupils away from the Puritan period and Arthur Miller's play – unless their act of deception can be carried out in the knowledge of the full horror of the cultural and religious rules they are choosing to break. This has to be the pivot of the scene.

With this in mind, I see a scene taking place in the town's meetinghouse or chapel, with me in role as the 'Minister' or 'Pastor', shocked at the rumours I have heard of dancing and witchcraft, inviting the families I have sent for whose houses border onto the woods, to send their off-spring to the altar rail to swear on the Bible that they are innocent. This act of deception will be an isolated action, carefully timed, public and formal. Pupils may begin to engage dramatically with an unfamiliar context if the structure of a scene draws on that context's *formal* rules.

This picture I have of a pivotal scene represents the beginning of my planning, but, typically of this kind of programme, it cannot necessarily be the beginning of the lesson itself. There are usually a number of steps emerging as preparation for such a scene. I will attempt to give an explanation of each step.

1. I talk briefly about Miller's play, mentioning that Puritans of the period feared many things, including the supernatural – rather like our superstitions today. I then laid out on the ground, far apart, five or more big sheets of blank paper around which pupils could group to make a rapid list of all the superstitions they could think of.

This is a useful releaser of class energy. Informally squatting on the floor they could just instruct their appointed 'scribe' to write whatever came into their heads, while they hear me, their teacher, half seriously, urge them to make a longer list than the next group. All light-hearted and fun – deliberately *not* striking a tone appropriate to the play.

2. I then ask them to walk round all the sheets, putting their initials by all the superstitions that they personally are sometimes affected by.

This 'signing one's name' is an act of commitment and also has bearing on Miller's play, when John Proctor, in the last Act, cannot give the authorities his *name*! As they sign, I ask them, casually and lightheartedly, to count the number of superstitions they identify with. We then do a count, laughingly starting with the highest number (I think 25 was the most!) and then going down to 3 or 2 or even 1 – and 'there may even be someone here who denies being affected by any of our list....' A chill creeps into my voice ... notice this '*our*' list, an *exclusive* and *excluding* touch. The one or two who have not signed anything are suddenly isolated ... not belonging to the rest of us ... different...' Come into the middle of the room and let the rest of us form a circle round you' ... 'We don't like people who are different...' I then invite the others to harass the isolates. (It only lasts a minute or so – I'm not a sadist!) I stop it, put my arms around the 'victims' and thank them for showing us what 'The Crucible' is about: 'This play is about gaining power by accusing people who seem to be different...'

3. All sitting in a circle now, I suddenly mime picking up a doll 'a poppet, as they called it in Salem...' I slowly lifted the doll's petticoats, narrating as I carried out the actions, and thrust a long needle deep into the doll's belly... 'for I have the power to curse as the children of Salem did, and if I wanted to curse someone I sent them this impaled poppet'. Again suddenly, I turned to my neighbour in the circle, thrust the 'doll' into his hands and instructed 'pass it on' – and when, eventually it came round to me again – I refused to take it.

Each child has a momentary public attention, as everyone watches how s/he receives and how s/he gives. A curse has descended on us! – and we have a feeling that 'theatre' has started.

4. Breaking the threatening mood, I invite the pupils to divide into family groups, limiting each family to two or three adolescent children. They are invited to think of themselves as a family portrait, a still picture which will not only convey the 'purity' of the off-springs and the father as 'head of family', but also, if they wish, the less than passive role of the mother, who, I suggested, might have more authority at home than the public image of the 'head of the household' embraces. Any such authority in a female member of the family must just be hinted at in this 'portrait'. The final responsibility for the portrait lies with the parents who are to try to make their children look like the most respectable and god-fearing children in Salem! I then, with each family formally facing inwards to the rest of the group, address each 'head of family' in turn, asking him to introduce each 'child' by name and to tell us whether each child has for example learnt to read the Bible aloud at meal-times.

This exercise is an example of a complex form of depiction, in which the participants prepare a still tableau for inspection which becomes elevated into a 'staged' performance of formalised, improvised, questions and answers *as though we are in the existential present.* This is, of course, a very stiff interchange, anticipating the rigidity of address needed for the 'chapel' scene and giving the class chance to test whether they are capable of treating such formalities with due seriousness. It also accustoms the pupils to the strategy of 'teacher-in-role'. (Notice this chance I give the girls playing 'mothers' to take on a more forceful role, albeit subtly, for when I first tried this sequence, I realised that it virtually leaves these girls out as 'passive onlookers', unless I give them a chance to find an important niche. Preparation for creating the portraits included a brief discussion about clothes – greys and blacks – hidden ankles and wrists and necks; daughters could use head-scarves so that 'not a thread of hair could be seen'.)

5. *'Parents, you may think, that your children are as innocent as you have made them look in this portraiture, but I have to tell you that, last night, round about midnight, some of your children were seen dancing naked in Salem woods – near your houses'. Having announced this, I then invite them to split up, inviting the 'parents' to leave the room while their 'children' write down, each on a slip of paper, the word GUILTY or INNOCENT. Then they show what they have written to each other and we have within this 'children' group a number who took part in last night's dancing and those who did not. I invite them to memorise which is which – and then I hint darkly that those who are guilty, who will be denying that guilt in the next scene, 'playing a part of the innocent', might like, at some point when it seems most favourable, to drop hints that bring the accusation of guilt on the wrong children, on the innocent! – just as in Miller's play.*

Notice this 'last night' – we are now into 'drama time'. Allowing the pupils to choose whether they want to be guilty or innocent is a very important part of the proceedings. It gives them a feeling of being in charge of themselves and it creates a 'real' secret from the actors playing the 'parents' who, in actuality, do not know which are the offending offspring.

6. *The chapel scene begins with the families entering and the 'minister' giving them permission to take their usual family seats in the 'House of God'. In my role I then give them the news of sacrilegious behaviour in the woods. I warn them of the wrath of God and speak of dire punishment. I then invite each*

'child' in turn to come forward, place a hand on the Bible (it has obviously to be not a Bible, of course – this is Drama) and say after me: 'My soul is pure'.

Thus they can 'be' those citizens of Salem, because the context is so tightly structured that at every moment behaviour is regulated by the cultural laws of the context and of the occasion. The actors have no room for manoeuvre within the the imposed strictures, but of course the greater the limitations the more subtle can be the creativity – and individual input was sometimes astonishingly inventive – within the 'rules of the Puritan game'. The restrictions are both safe and constructive. It is the deep values of the culture that are dictating behaviour not 'personality'. The 'plot' for the scene was that the pastor had sent for the families – even though it was week-day and harvesting time – and they had had to change into their stiff 'chapel best'.

7. The 'minister' now instructs each family to seek privacy in one of the many chapel vestries in order to interrogate the children and 'get them to confess' so that they may be publicly admonished.

This is the most testing part of the whole session. If the previous steps have not been handled well, this scene, which requires small family groups to operate separately with the 'parents' taking charge (replacing the 'teacher-in-role' function of the teacher, as it were) will collapse. The security of the previous scene is replaced with *too much* room for manoeuvering in this one. Only if the pupils are by now committed and if the 'parents' take on their responsibility is it going to work. My role is, of course, still available to intervene as the 'Minister just going round the vestries to see if anyone has confessed', should it be necessary. If all goes well, one or two innocent people will be 'named'!

8. Final scene, back in the chapel, in which the Minister invites confessions, and, just as in 'The Crucible', accusations. This scene may go in any direction. At its best, the class take over and the 'Minister' plays a minor role in the ways things are handled.

This handing over of power to the class is of course very important and cannot always be achieved within one session. In this particular lesson, such class autonomy is built into the plan. If it works well, the pupils will not only be trying to think inside the Puritan situation, but also trying to adopt a kind of stylised language to accompany their posturing.

9. Outside the drama, the 'children' reveal the truth! – and there is much laughter for many of the 'parents' were genuinely deceived.

A sign of a worthwhile drama experience at this point is whether the pupils, out of role, feel an urge to talk about it to each other. If your class remains respectfully silent, waiting for you to tell them what to do next, something has gone very wrong! – and this happened to me on one occasion. Mostly however, this sequence seems to have all the ingredients that make for good 'theatre' – and creates an eagerness to turn to Miller's text.

I showed the full plan of this 'Crucible' lesson to Dorothy Heathcote whose reaction was to applaud its intention but to express doubt about the viability of using direct improvisation (that is, an improvisation where the pupils attempt to become characters from a text) in relation to a text about to be studied. She saw a danger of such a 'dramatic experience' becoming so attractive in itself without any guarantee that it be true to the text. In thinking about what *she* would do, her mind immediately turned to the question of how the pupils should be *framed.*

Research into 'living through' Drama by Peter Millward

I have suggested that the above accounts of practice by Bolton and O'Neill, respectively, represent a re-interpretation of 'living through' practice, but in attempting to give instances from Heathcote's practice in the previous chapter, I may have lost sight of its definitive character. One of the confusions is that although the words 'living through' imply that important sense of 'being there in the present and presence', Heathcote's methodology also builds in its opposite of 'being outside it'. There is a mercurial inside-outside dialectic that heightens awareness. Thus 'living through' implies continually arresting the process of living to take a look at it, and it is the *spectator* as much as the *participant* that re-engages with that *living.*

We will now look at Peter Millward's (1988) account of his own unique experimentation in 'living through'. It is unique in a number of respects, one being that he did not intend, when he set up the experiment, that it should turn into drama. His initial interest was in how eight-year old children contribute to a discussion and for this purpose arranged to have a teacher colleague take a mixed ability group of six children to an empty staff room so that Millward could sound record the proceedings. What started as a discussion on volcanoes Millward suddenly took over simply because '...it felt right'. Even when the recording of this tentative venture into drama was over, Millward did not immediately see it as a basis for his research. However, *three months later,* he invites the same six children to continue the drama from where they had left off, which they do with only a modicum of prompting from Millward. For the first recording, the children and the the original teacher (who took no part in the drama) continued to sit round a staffroom table as they 'slipped into' drama. For the second recording, they moved around in a chosen space in the hall. Throughout both recordings Millward was in role. Thus the data for this research is uniquely a record of the dialogue that emerged from the inter- actions of a teacher and just six pupils in a fiction-making context, the topic of which was ostensibly 'living under a volcano', an extension of what they had been discussing. The teacher had no preconceptions of where it was going and certainly no notion of teaching the six something about volcanoes.

We have a complete recording, then, of an unassuming, unsophisticated ver- sion of 'living through' Drama. In addition, we have Millward's penetrating analysis from an ethnomethodological perspective. Millward gives us both an unpretentious, 'pure' example of 'living through' drama and a way of talking about it that is of critical interest to this study.

The Drama
Having asked permission to interrupt the discussion Millward finds himself saying:

Teacher	Can you imagine that each of you... are [sic] a person who lives in a little village by a volcano, all right? And I'm a stranger and I'm coming to talk to you. All right?
All	Mmm
Teacher	Can you do that from this moment? Stop being yourselves for a moment, well, be yourselves... but [laughter] be yourselves in this village.
Ian	Mmm
Teacher	All right?
All	Mmm

Deceptively fumbling, Millward invites his group of six to stumble with him into living beneath a volcano, interrupting a discussion on what it must be like for people living in such circumstances. The 'fumbling' of course is this teacher's way of ensuring that what ensues is 'living through'. He could have said, 'This has been a very interesting discussion; shall we turn it into a play?' Millward believes there are two traps in such a question. Firstly, the 'we' ('shall we turn it into a play) reinforces the framework of 'a teacher and six pupils' for in that staffroom that is who they are. Having engaged in discussion they (the said 'teacher and pupils') would have then switched to a different 'teacher and pupils' task, that is, – making up a drama. According to Millward, 'Pupils doing drama' about volcano living is of a different order from 'living under a volcano'. Hence Millward's deliberate 'Stop being yourselves ... well, be yourselves in this village' muddle. It is his way of saying *Be here now*'. They are not to '*do drama*' but to 'present experience dramatically'. Of course they will continue to be pupils with a teacher and the school staffroom will remain as a stubborn reminder of who they are and where they are, but in the 'dramatic presentation of experience' such a school framework may fade (but never entirely disappear) in favour of the new framework of people living here, at the foot of a dangerous mountain.

Secondly, making a play about people who live beneath a volcano traps the class into an unhelpful assumption about the nature of drama. Peter Millward has pointed out that writers on drama education are misleading when they imply that the meaning of drama lies in its faithful representation of a 'real' world. Such writers do not always take care to distinguish between drama as an experience in its own right and drama as a duplication. 'Shall we turn our discussion into a play?' appears to be inviting a class to consider people who live beneath volcanoes and *represent* their lives by imitating them as best we can. This would, in Millward's terms, be '*doing drama*', drawing on an imitative talent that does not belong to 'living through'. Thus the two traps within the question, 'Shall we do a play about people living beneath a volcano?' relate to *who* (teacher and pupils) and *what* (representation of those volcano people).

Millward could, of course, have chosen to invite the six children to 'just play' at living underneath a volcano, clearing a space in the staffroom for them to do so. Assuming they were capable or motivated to be so engaged, this would have amounted to what I have defined above as 'dramatic playing'. For Millward, however, this was not an alternative choice. Straightaway he brings in teacher-in-role, a dimension, as we have seen, critical to 'living through'. His choice of role ('And I'll be a stranger and I'm coming to talk to you') is highly significant at a number of levels affecting the ensuing drama. Three will be discussed below.

(1) 'And I'm coming to talk to you' deftly takes them into the drama without a break, for talking is what he is already doing, so that when he continues with:

Teacher	You know, what I can't understand ... is, being a stranger and not living in a place like this little village which you live in with that great volcano smoking away all day ... what I can't understand is why you

> still stay here... why do you keep your village down
> here below this great volcano?

They, the children, are able to continue sitting in their chairs 'hearing' that they are somewhere else and no doubt 'seeing' the 'stranger's' uplifted nod in the direction of something towering above them. Only in the second session of this drama, three months later, do the six 'get on their feet'. This sedentary acting behaviour represents a huge contrast with the Stone/Slade/Way 'physical education' starting-point for drama work. All that appears to be necessary for drama of this kind is a token physicality (in this instance the upward movement of the stranger's eyes). Necessary, but obviously not always sufficient, for we shall see actions later take on central importance.

(2) By taking on a role of someone who may ask questions Millward appears here to be perpetuating 'the power teachers have over children' and exercising his teacher 'rights' to ask questions. The diffident style of the teacher's language, however, is sufficient to signal that the social context has changed. Just as the *physical* change was virtually nonexistent, so the structural aspect of 'teacher asking questions to which children answer' has not changed. What has changed is this teacher's whole demeanour including his choice of paralinguistic signals. The first two dimensions, the physical and the structural components, keep the children anchored in a school setting; it is the *style* of presentation, illuminating 'stranger' and 'village dwellers' that appears to be just sufficient, at this testing moment of opening up a 'living through' drama, to help the children present their experience dramatically. Only just sufficient, for after a four second silence from the class, one boy risks 'You get plenty of water', an answer, as Millward points out, safely poised between two structures, for such an answer cleverly satisfies both 'pupil responding to teacher' and 'villager responding to stranger' contexts. The same boy's subsequent generalisation ('There's water in the ground in some volcanoes') suggests a reversion to the former context, but the 'stranger's 'Do you all have hot water in your huts?' now throws out a challenge to establish a 'volcano' context in which they can no longer cling to being pupils in a staffroom... 'Yes', they answer in turn – and when, to the teacher's follow up question, 'Has any of you [*and here the 'stranger' adopts a newly serious tone*] ever had a ... close friend... hurt... or even killed by the volcano?', one girl affirms that this is the case, they are suddenly people endowed with a past history – and there is no going back.

3. We have seen that an important part of Dorothy Heathcote's management of 'living through' drama is her constant departure from role in order to get a

class to reflect and dig deeper into what they are creating. Peter Millward has chosen one of the few roles open to a teacher that has its own built-in reflection device, for as a 'stranger' he can pose questions at an ever deepening level and, equally important to 'living through' drama, his 'strangerness' inherently contributes to creating an image of the children as a community, for his role is a catalyst to their collective role. His 'strangerness' to a community provides the natural dynamic for giving it an identity, which the rest of the dialogue proceeds to do. From 'past injury', the questions and answers between stranger and villagers moved to 'thoughts of climbing the volcano', which the children turn into a taboo, for reasons to do with 'jewels at the top' ('*you can see 'em glittering at night*'), which turn out to be a '*sign of the great god*' ...who turns climbers into victims... kept '*in the heart, the heart of the volcano*'. To the teacher's question 'How do you know he (the great god) put them there?', one of the answers is 'We just believe in him'. Others know he is there, '*cause you see him on a night... his... great crown in the sky... against the sky*'. All of which speedily, but with no prompting from the teacher, turns into a drama in which, before 'high priests' the 'stranger' is challenged with '*Have you learnt the great laws?*'

Thus in a response to a teacher whose mind was pursuing matters of practical significance to do with constant hot water and climbers getting hurt, the children take their play into mystical and canonical realms. They are penetrating into a community's values – and it is the teacher's choice of role that has created the opportunity to do so. Everything they do subsequently in their 'living through' is sustained by this deeper commitment, which they have to work hard to maintain. The ethnomethodological theory adopted by Millward (and by me in so far as it helps distinguish between 'living through' drama and 'doing a play') is of social experience as a managed accomplishment, of social life existing 'in the manner through which we attend to it'. His purpose is to extend that theory to embrace drama. He argues that just as there is tacit agreement among those involved in a social situation to make that situation meaningful through their talk and actions, so people participating in presenting experience dramatically honour the same agreement and draw on the same kind of 'common knowledge' to make the dramatic situation meaningful. In the everyday presentation of experience, meaning is located in the work done by those involved to give their experience stability and character so that it may appear to themselves and others as real.

The above fits very well too as a description 'living through' drama. Only when something goes wrong in our everyday management of social experience are we made to be aware of this collaborative effort. In 'living through' drama, however, we are conscious of what we are doing; we know that it is make-believe and therefore without the consequences of everyday experience, but it is meaningful as everyday experience is meaningful, in that the way we work at it is, reflexively, a constituent part of its meaning. The dramatic context is not a 'given' to be enacted (as in 'doing drama'); it is a managed accomplishment to be treated, as for any social context, 'as real'. If social life can be described, as Rom Harré (1983) does, as 'a kind of conversation' (p129), so can 'living through' drama, for they are both dependent on a shared frame of mind, generated from the same resources, composed of the same elements, and made effective through communication and interpretation. Both 'living through drama' (along with the dramatic playing of children without a teacher) and everyday experience are wrought from the efforts of the participants. They may draw on familiar patterns of social codes, but each moment is newly forged. In the 'volcano drama' the children work at making sense of the contingency of their inventions – testing a stranger, guarding their treasures and beliefs etc. Because it is make-believe, their universe is hugely enlarged and they knowingly invent their 'new conversation'.

Just before the second phase of their drama (three months later), Millward injected a dramatic tension into the work. The children had already evolved a situation in which two of the children were in role as guides to the 'stranger' encouraging and helping him to climb the mountain, whereas two others were disapproving of the 'stranger', and disapproving of his taking the test. Millward, outside the drama, encouraged the latter to behave, however, as if they had the stranger's 'best interests' at heart. With this ploy, of course, Millward is straying from Heathcote's refined version of 'living through' to unashamed 'Man in a Mess' (in this instance it is the *stranger* in the Mess!), but one can sense the huge enjoyment and sense of power the children gained from the subtle deception. At one point in the sequence, it is thought necessary by the 'guardians' that the 'stranger' should meet their father, a 'blind man' whose disability, so it emerged, had been caused by doing the same 'test'. ... Millward's class of six young children create blindness out of dialogue, as a playwright would. It is not the boy playing the 'blind father' who has to work to portray that role. ... His blindness is established by the very way people tend to present disability in a social context:

> Mark: Ah, here he is now (said as though the man cannot present himself). Come on... careful... over here... come on...
>
> Julia: Mind the steps.
>
> Mark: Careful...careful down.

Julia: One more. There you are. We'll get you a seat.

Mark: He's made it now, as you can see.

Julia: There you are. Sit down on there.

Mark: Sit down. Right ... he made it here.

Here is a remarkable example of how a particular person's handicap is not his alone, but also 'other people's perceptions' of a person with a handicap, as Millward puts it. The others speak of the blind man as though he were not there, quite incapable of speaking for himself. Thus they are meeting *two* objectives. Making blindness visible is part of presenting the social structure, but at the same time, they are conscious that by doing so they are moving their drama along, for that 'stranger' will be made more and more uncomfortable by the evidence of this blind man's failure to pass the test unscathed.

The 'teacher/pupil' structure has faded even more into the background, as they confidently make sense of what is going on and also see what is going on as a drama. Their drama-making has at least two aspects: their dialogue becomes more publicly viable as they acquire a stronger sense of spectatorship towards what they are creating; and the structure of what they are creating becomes closely allied to a well-made play. Peter Millward demonstrates how dramatist's skills of handling beginnings, endings, entrances, dramatic irony, symbolism and sub-texts etc. are part and parcel of these eight year olds' dramatic repertoire. Millward warns us that we should not be beguiled into assuming that these beautifully managed constructions are stored up in their minds as calculated effects waiting to be expressed. They *discover* what they are doing as they do it. This is artistic spontaneity, grounded in understanding of what is needed, at its best. The meaningfulness of the event inheres in itself, without reference to some 'real' world out there or to some preconceived script or to some previous discussion. 'Living through' drama essentially operates from *inside* the event; there is no model of fact or form, nor is there any felt need to maintain the 'teacher's and pupils' social structure. Its defining component, however, is 'teacher-in-role'. Peter Millward just followed the direction the children took; in doing so he *honoured* their creativity. When it seemed appropriate, from outside the drama he guaranteed dramatic irony by encouraging a theatrical deception, and then he continued to follow.

Towards a conceptual framework for classroom acting behaviour

This is Chapter 11, in its entirety, from *Acting in Classroom Drama* (1998). It is the culmination of the thesis of the book which argues that the mode of involvement in classroom drama, which necessitates that children creating themselves in the here and now of a 'living through' experience, is a unique form of drama involvement, qualitatively different from stage acting. He calls this whole process *making* drama.

This publication, and this final chapter in particular, is trying to outline a conceptual framework which could allow teachers adopting an eclectic approach to communicate with each other by sharing a common language. By common language, I do not mean common vocabulary or terminology. My choice of labels for categories is quite arbitrary. It matters not whether we choose to name, say, the acting required for a tableau as 'showing' or 'presenting' or 'demonstrating' or whatever – I have chosen, as it happens, to call it 'presenting'. What does matter is that teachers can *share the conception* of a mode of acting as a definable category and see such a classification as serving a useful purpose.

A central problem in attempting to categorise behaviours of any kind is to determine what level of categorisation would have the most practical use. The danger is that we fall in love with *differences* and indulgently spin out innumerable classifications – a good time could be had taking each illustration of practice of the previous chapters of this book and, slotting each into a category of its own, and still have categories left over! At the other extreme is the temptation to ignore differences entirely and go for samenesses – and to ones delight one finds that there is only *one category. All acting is the same!*

It is this latter trap that David Hornbrook (1989) has fallen into when he writes, 'It is my contention that conceptually there is nothing which differentiates the child acting in the classroom from the actor on the stage of the theatre' (p104). And, of course, *at the conceptual level he has chosen to operate*

19

he is right. The first part of this chapter will appear to demonstrate just how right he is, for I shall begin by studying what acting behaviours share in common. Attractive as this may be, how *useful* is it? Is there, therefore, a *minimum* number of categories which could show essential differences at a fundamental level while retaining this important sense of *oneness*, for one can appreciate what persuaded Hornbrook to overstate similarities – much of the history outlined in this book has been about people failing to recognise common ground.

I have kept my classification to a minimum of three major categories, or rather, two major categories and a powerful sub category – after which confusing statement – I can only hope that the basis for my divisions will become clear towards the end of this chapter.

Common ground of all classroom acting behaviours

The account of the work of five pioneers and other leading exponents of classroom drama has revealed many different kinds of activities executed in the name of drama, but 'entry into fiction' is what they (mostly) share. I wish to argue that other common ground includes the mimetic, aesthetic, generalising, communicating and focusing features commonly associated with acting.

A psychological feature common to all acting behaviours: The tension between imitating and inventing

I began this study with John Allen's (1979) translation of Aristotle's 'Mimesis' as an 'act of recreation', a term suggesting invention as well as imitation. The story of this century's drama teaching reveals marked contrasts in the degree and kind of imitation involved. Irene Mawer's (1932) 'practice in walking like kings and queens', for instance, represents an extreme version of imitative behaviour required by a teacher of her pupils, as Peter Millward's (1988) deliberately ambiguous instruction to his class '...stop being yourselves for a moment, well be yourselves... but be yourselves in this village...' seemingly precludes imitation; 'seemingly', for, as we shall argue later in this chapter, any form of enactment requires a public medium sufficiently referential to be understood by others. I have earlier quoted from Ernst Cassirer (1953) who captures the tension between imitating and inventing: '...reproduction never consists in retracing, line for line, a specific content of reality; but in selecting a pregnant motif.'

However, there seems to be a cluster of terms used by writers to explain the two-pronged psychological relationship between the actor and the 'real' world and between the actor and the fiction. I want to suggest that **Identifica-**

tion may be a useful umbrella term under which the imitative/inventive tension of 'Mimesis' could be subsumed along with other recurring characteristics. I have already favoured 'identification' over Peter Slade's and others' insistence on 'sincerity' as a prerequisite for Child Drama. Indeed I defined the process of identification in terms that simultaneously expand both on 'Sincerity' and 'Mimesis': 'The child abstracts a 'truth' from the situation as s/he sees it for the purpose of representation. What is represented is the child's understanding of, not a facsimile of, a reality.' I have written 'child' here, as I am concentrating on classroom behaviour, but the same could be said of the actor on stage, or, indeed of one of Caldwell Cook's 'players' who offers, not Hamlet, but his understanding of Hamlet expressed through an act of *interpretation*. It may be dualistic to suggest in this way that the player's 'interpretation' *reflects* his 'understanding', implying two discrete stages of a temporal sequence, as though, having (internally) 'understood' Hamlet, he *then* proceeds (externally) to 'interpret' him. Nevertheless, it seems important to the practice of drama to give a place to the notion that there may be a mismatch between understanding and interpretation, that, for instance, an act of interpretation may, through lack of skill or commitment, fall short of a person's understanding, or, conversely, that engagement in an act of interpretation may itself extend the understanding.

To link the *inventive* face of Mimesis solely with 'interpretation', however, is to concentrate on its intellectual aspect, whereas a central feature of acting behaviour is its potential for spontaneity, a quality the Psychodramatist, J.L. Moreno, experimented with in his patients as early as 1922 when he set up the first 'Therapeutic Theatre' in Vienna. Most of the educationists supporting the notion of improvised drama have valued it for its immediacy. There seems to have been an assumption that 'spontaneous' was synonymous with 'creative'. Brian Way built his whole theory of education on the importance of intuition as opposed to intellect. Even working on a Chamber Theatre script, Dorothy Heathcote insists that the players 'discover on their feet' the best way to convey the multiple meanings of the text. According to Shomit Mitter, Stanislavski, towards the end of his career, refound his faith in the somatic and advised his actors to 'start bravely, not to reason, but to act'. Perhaps the antithesis of imitation is best expressed in the term 'disponibilite', described by Frost and Yarrow as 'a kind of total awareness, a sense of being at one with the context: (with a) script, if such there be, actors, audience, theatre space, oneself and one's body.' [...]

Only if 'identification' can embrace the notion of spontaneity as an essential part of Mimesis is it useful to us as an umbrella term. Identification must imply a sufficient capacity for ownership of the fiction to allow free play within both the interpretation and 'the moment of it happening'.

Thus, in the context of acting behaviour, 'identification' stands for a many-stranded, radial connection between a person and the 'real world' *and* between that person and the fiction created, involving 'understanding', 'imitation', 'individual interpretation', 'group consensus', 'commitment', 'sincerity', and 'disponibilite'. John O'Toole (1992) writes of the *quality* and *degree* of identification, treating them almost synonymously, and suggesting they will vary according to commitment, maturity, and dramatic skill. An implication here is that quality of identification is objectively assessable. This may be so, but it seems also to be the case that even ill-informed identification may remain 'true' for the participant and, further, the *degree* or intensity of the identification may be relatively high in spite of inadequate information or knowledge. The possibility of a direct correspondence between degree and quality of identification remains in doubt.

John O'Toole draws our attention to a source of commitment in fiction-making that may sometimes override all other factors, in which the vested interest in the content of the drama by the participants is explicitly expressive of their 'real world'. O'Toole cites an example from my teaching in South Africa in 1980, made dramatic in both a fictitious and real sense by a black boy, towards the end of the improvised drama, taking my hand (he, in role as an old man living in the year 2050 and I in role as a 'white journalist'), and saying as he shook it, 'We are equal now'. Such a moment of 'identification' was 'true for us', 'spontaneous', and 'committed', but not necessarily dependent on dramatic skill, or, for my part, on extensive knowledge.

I have suggested that 'fiction' is the nucleus of all acting behaviour. It is possible now to see 'identification' as a further defining feature, so that a definition of acting behaviour would so far read as **fiction-making involving identification through action**. It is not meant to suggest, as Morgan and Saxton (1991) (with a different purpose in mind) do, that the extent or depth of identification is paralleled by a matching complexity in level of action, but rather that maximum identification may be expressed in any kind of acting behaviour, whether it be the child described by Piaget who put her doll on an imaginary tractor because she is afraid of the tractor in the neighbouring field, or the ten year old boy in Heathcote's 'Making History' series who confronts the 'villeins' with 'You do not understand why this book is so important to us. It's part of our life. We need it so much. It's what our Lord said', or Finlay-Johnson's pupils who were 'so exceedingly good' as Rosalind and Celia. Just as the degree of identification does not determine its *quality*, so the intensity of identification does not determine the *kind* of acting behaviour, nor, conversely, can it be assumed that one kind of acting behaviour will guarantee a higher degree of intensity than another.

Degree or intensity of identification does, however, determine whether or not make-believe can occur. A major problem emerging from Marjorie Hourd's, Peter Slade's and Dorothy Heathcote's approaches, for example, has been the one of 'ownership' in the early stages of, respectively, Hourd's invitation to 'do the accompanying actions to a ballad', Slade's narration of a made-up story and Heathcote's use of teacher-in-role. Each of these exponents' methodologies, depends for its success on relinquishing the teacher's ownership of the fiction to their pupils while relying on considerable external input – a poem in (possibly) obscure language from Hourd; a series of teacher-timed instructions from Slade and a powerful acting display from Heathcote – and it is possible that none of these sufficiently capture the imagination of some children in their classes and that consequently their commitment remains too low for engagement with the fiction. On the other hand, in Hourd's classroom the poem may capture the child's imagination, but the techniques and personal exposure required to represent it in Mime may seem formidable. These are but examples from particular methodologies, but the problem of appropriate level of commitment is a feature of all acting behaviours.

An aesthetic feature common to all acting behaviours: Fictitious time and space

If we search the publications of our pioneers and other leading figures for selected images of what they might have considered to be among the principal aesthetic features of classroom acting behaviour, we find in Harriet Finlay-Johnson (1911) a high tolerance for 'crude action' combined with a penchant for representational realism in costume, properties and scenery; Henry Caldwell Cook (1917) sought an intelligent use of the spatial proportions of an Elizabethan stage and the avoidance of realism; for Jacques-Dalcroze (1921) 'rhythm' created the basis for all the arts and he introduces the concept of 'musical gesture'; Irene Mawer (1932) emphasised mental and muscular control, physical fitness and imagination; Frances Mackenzie (1935) insisted on the importance of the use of the voice, facial expression, timing, holding pauses and effective exits; Robert Newton (1937) was concerned with 'form', by which he meant elements of surprise, contrast, mood and climax; Langdon (1949) saw the shape of the dramatic event, the plot, beginnings and endings and climax, as its key components; Marjorie Hourd

(1949) sought 'naturalism', by which she meant an untutored, unself-conscious, 'statuary' style of acting, as her pupils discovered the actions to accompany a ballad; Peter Stone (1949) introduced 'movement for movement's sake', in the physical training space of the school hall; Peter Slade (1954) believed in a spatial/musical dimension that could reach heights of artistry; Brian Way (1967) favoured individual practice of actions to music, stimulating the pupil's image-making. Dorothy Heathcote (1995) pursues significance in the use of the theatrical elements of sound/silence, movement/stillness/and light/darkness; and Cecily O'Neill (1995) seeks dramatic irony. Such a collection of images may not entirely do justice to the individuals referred to, but they serve to give an overall picture of a range of aesthetic priorities pointing to considerable conceptual differences.

One aesthetic aspect they have in common, however, is a manipulation of time and space. The relationship of acting behaviour to time and space is of a different order from everyday actions to time and space, from what Schechner (1982) more poetically, if depressingly, calls 'the flux and decay of ongoing living'. Acting behaviour is dependent upon, yet *outside* or *bracketed from* the time/space dimensions. Bateson's (1976) analogy of 'picture frame' and 'wallpaper' which he used to demonstrate a different order of meanings within 'play' and 'not play' activities may, I believe, be extended. Whereas his argument pertained to the 'denotation', and 'interpretation' of what was going on within the frame (as opposed to the wallpaper on which the frame is hung), I suggest the same metaphor could be applied to a 'player's' perception of 'time' and 'space' within the frame. The 'here and now' of acting is not the 'here and now' of existing. Schechner (1977) captures something of the difference when he says:

> Theater [sic], to be effective, must maintain its double or incomplete presence, as *a here-and-now performance of there-and-then events*. The gap between the 'here and now' and 'there and then' allows an audience to contemplate the action, and to entertain alternatives.

Again, Schechner's focus, while seeing time and space as critical elements, is ultimately concerned with the meanings to be extracted and interpreted by an imaginative audience. I am interested here in establishing that this 'double and incomplete presence' requires the actor to be in the 'here and now', but, as it were, *outside* the bracket, *playing* with the 'here and now' inside the bracket. A vivid example of such 'playing with time and space' can be seen in Bertolt Brecht's (1949) instruction to his actors that in rehearsing a text they should render it:

not as an improvisation, but as a *quotation*. At the same time it is clear that he has to render, in this quotation, all the undertones, all the concrete, plastic detail of human utterance. His gestures, though they are frankly a *copy* (and not spontaneous), must have the full corporeality of human gestures. (p39)

In this example the actor is astride two time/space dimensions. He is located in space and existing 'in present time' and yet conveying implicitly, through 'quotation', a third person and a past time. In Chamber theatre, as we have seen, the *elasticity* of the time/space dimension is harnessed explicitly. Most 'living through' drama enjoys considerable freedom in time/space manipulation.

And yet in the first part of Peter Millward's experimental drama, action was avoided altogether. 'Why do you keep your village down here below this great volcano?', from teacher fumbling with his role as stranger, hardly seems to invite action of any kind. In fact, as we have already seen, he is addressing six children round a table in the staff-room – and that is where they stay for the whole of that first session. Does this qualify as drama? Where does this stand in relation to a theory that all acting behaviour is dependent on 'bracketed' time and space? In this episode action seems to have been reduced out of existence, but nevertheless a fictitious time and space are *implied*. That is not to suggest that incipient action is present: there is a huge gap between being round that table and the actions of living in that village; it would have required a very brave soul (and perhaps one insensitive to the medium) to have started doing 'volcanic village actions'. We have, therefore, a special kind of manipulation of time and space. Those dimensions grew and were 'played with' *in their minds* and did not become evident until the second session three months later. Thus the definition of acting behaviour as 'fiction-making involving identification through action' should be understood to embrace *implied* or *mental* action.

What is not brought out by Millward's thesis is the notion of double space/ time dimensions. Part of being in the fiction is the chance to play with time and space, so that the most literal gesture, coinciding exactly with how it would be done in 'real life' in terms of time, space and energy, is done that way by *choice*; the participant is still outside the time/space bracket while deploying the dimensions within it. When Millward's pupils move into the school hall, space is immediately manipulated by giving status to the 'priest's place' outside which 'shoes have to be removed', but time runs at a conversational pace until slowed down by the ceremony of 'meeting the priests' and we then, and only then, become aware of time and space being deftly handled to give meaning to their creation. When, out of choice, their timing and 'spacing' co-incide with an everyday, 'conversational' usage, we are not aware of it as manipulation from 'outside the bracket'.

It is interesting that Dorothy Heathcote, the one writer who explicitly offers us an image of the manipulation of the three dimensions of 'space', 'time' and 'light' as central to her work should also present us with the greatest problem when it comes to trying to fit that image into her later practice, 'Mantle of the Expert'. Mostly her pupils are carrying out tasks in a way that suggests they are 'inside the bracket'. They are doing 'literal' tasks requiring 'everyday' timing – they are discussing, drawing, recording, cutting out, measuring, looking something up etc etc. Drawing a map demands the same spatial/ temporal dimensions whether or not one is in a role as 'expert'. Set against this, how-ever, in 'Mantle of the Expert', we have another example of implied fictitious dimensions: just as a tilt of the head could suggest 'a volcano up there' in Millward's first session, so a glance at the the desk in the classroom corner indicates where you go to discuss a problem with the 'manager'; on the wall is the staff 'holiday' roster'; over the door shows the firm was established in 1907; and your 'Personal File' shows you have been an employee here for two years nine months. The whole activity is suffused with fictitious time while operating in the obstinate present of 'having in *actuality* to finish that map'. Nevertheless, traditional views of drama become challenged by the 'Mantle of the Expert' task-centred approach because it is traditionally assumed, by theatre theorists and child play theorists alike, that any 'character' drawing a map as part of 'a Play' or in 'Playing' will but *indicate* the action.

We can now add this time-space dimension to our definition of 'acting be-haviour: **it is an act of fiction-making involving identification through action and the conscious manipulation of time and space**. I believe this definition applies across the range of classroom drama.

'Acting as generalisation' in all acting behaviours

That acting behaviour manipulates time/space from outside the bracket re-inforces the notion, first introduced into education literature by Susan Isaacs (1933), that make believe play enables 'the emancipation of meanings from the here and now of a concrete situation.' Drama as a medium for education is based on this capacity for generalisation from its particularity. The 'bracket-ing' of action invites that action to be attended to 'as' action, of interest 'beyond itself', as Lars Kleberg (1993) has expressed it. Put succinctly: as well as being 'as if ', drama essentially is 'as'. This theoretical aspect is once again challenged by the 'Mantle of the Expert' role. Mantle of the Expert's reliance on *actual* behaviours seems, in this respect, to disqualify it as dramatic, although, of course, like geysers bursting out of a plateau, the most obviously dramatic structures of 'depicting', 'replaying the past' 'anticipating the future' and 'Chamber Theatre' etc are as integral to 'Mantle of the Expert' as the task work. But they belong to the second dimension of Mantle of the Expert. It is as though, although wearing the expert mantle, *drama* doesn't start for Heathcote's pupils until they are involved in drama-like contexts such as, say, 'setting up an interview with a customer'. To some extent this is paralleled by Caldwell Cook's (1917) pupils who see themselves as *players* but are not involved in drama until they actually start performing.

Thus our definition might now read: **Acting behaviour is an act of fiction-making involving identification through action, the conscious manipulation of time and space and a capacity for generalisation.**

The concept of 'audience' as a feature common to all acting behaviours

Interest in whether or not there should be an audience has been a major thread running through this history of drama teaching amounting, almost, to a plot-filled story of exponents' preferences. Finlay-Johnson (1911) wrote of 'doing away with an audience', by giving them responsibilities; Caldwell Cook's whole approach was with an audience in mind, developing what I have designated a 'platform' mentality; for Susan Isaacs' research of the play of her infants only observers were present; Langdon saw the presence or absence of spectators as a developmental issue – with no audience for infants, 'playing it out with an audience there' for lower Juniors and beginning to understand 'the rights of an audience' for the older ones; Mackenzie (1935), Mawer (1932) and Newton (1937) saw their work as entirely audience orientated as did the speech teachers of the 1920s and 30s; Hourd, like her colleague, Langdon, saw it as a developmental matter but interestingly perceived Junior school children (provided they were not turned into 'conscious artists') as stronger candidates for public performance than lower adolescents; Stone (1949), Slade (1954) and Way (1967) banished the idea of an audience, although Way does accept that small groups showing each other their work may be inevitable, if regrettable; Burton (1949) urged that the audience should 'know what we are experiencing'. The Schools Council (1977), while recognising the significant 'shift of emphasis' between 'acting-out' and 'performing', saw it as a matter of 'readiness'. Robinson (1980) makes a clear distinction between 'exploratory activities of classroom drama' and 'the activities of those who act a part to an audience.' Heathcote's (1995) teaching shows little interest in a traditional audience, but nevertheless generates a strong 'sense' of audience; in Millward's (1988) work an audience would have been irrelevant; O'Neill's (1995) 'Process Drama' includes, selectively, opportunities for rehearsal, with or without texts, and intense audience observation.

To argue as I have done above for 'manipulating time and space' as the common ground in spite of so many obvious differences in practice may seem to have challenged conventional wisdom. It may seem even more perverse to now argue in the light of the contradictory list in the preceding paragraph that *audience* is a common factor in classroom drama practice. However, I believe it to be important to do so.

It will be my purpose within the next few pages to replace the audience/no audience division with a tripartite classification based on the orientation of the players. In other words, in order to establish 'audience' as a *common* factor in all classroom drama, we shall be required to neutralise some of its related dichotomies and at the same time introduce an alternative classification.

The concept of audience: 'Public/Private' dichotomies

This dichotomy is to be found in the writings of James Sully (1896) who draws a distinction between the 'contented privacy' of child play and the public face of art. In the history of drama education and professional theatre there have been two meanings applied to the notion of 'privacy'. One is linked with the need for protection from public scrutiny at times of vulnerability, such as many theatre directors guarantee their actors during rehearsals and when Peter Stone insists that only selected guests may be brought in to observe the work. The other, relating to linguistics or semiotics, raises an important philosophical issue. Part of the progressive movement's ideology is the notion of an 'inner self' whose expression remains private, personal and inaccessible to others. Among the drama exponents, Slade and Way most notably, take this position, one which David Best argues is untenable. He avers that not only is an individual's means of expression dependent on culturally determined media, it is the media (particularly language and the arts) that determine the kinds of thoughts and feelings he is capable of having in the first place. In other words, all forms of expression are potentially 'public' because they are culturally derived.

If we take an example of classroom drama that clearly showed no interest in entertaining an outside audience, such as Millward's 'Volcano Drama', in the light of Best's theory, we can see that the young pupils' struggle to 'present experience dramatically' (to use Millward's phrase), has little to do with idiosyncratic, individual expression, but, rather, its opposite. They are seeking a *public* agreement about what is going on – and they are 'audience' to each others' endeavours.

The concept of audience: 'Process/Product' dichotomy

Caldwell Cook saw the value of his broad 'playway' in terms both of 'destination' and 'journey', the latter, he insisted, to have the greater claim. The first writer to make a precise distinction between 'process' and 'product' in classroom drama was E.M. Langdon (1949) who drew on a grammatical analogy of 'playing' and a 'play', which she used synonymously with 'pretending' and 'acting'. She saw the infant age group as the province of the former in preparation for a gradual change to the latter in the Junior school. The first was to be without an audience and the second was to go through a phase of 'playing it out with an audience there' and beginning to recognise 'the rights of an audience'. Exponents may have disagreed over the age groups, but Langdon's division into 'playing' and 'a play' is a thesis many have found acceptable. Just as the rehearsal process is seen as an opportunity for actors to explore and experiment without penalty, so 'playing' is seen as an essential element of improvised classroom drama. At its weakest it is intended to be regarded as exploratory, not 'public', and therefore not subject to critical appraisal; at its best it is intended to be regarded as a 'public', spontaneous, meaningful, dramatic presentation of experience, having, as in Millward's work, 'all the makings of a well-made play'.

It has made sense to a large number of drama teachers to emphasise the value of this kind of process for itself. The experimentation, risk-taking and discoveries involved have been seen as integral to personal development, whether the methodology be stage or child or content centred. It may be mistaken, however, to leave the impression, as some writers have done, that 'process' is to be seen as an alternative to 'product', for they are *interdependent*, not polar, concepts. Fleming (1994) expresses it succinctly: 'For in an active discipline like drama every end product contains a process within it and every process is in some sense a product.' As he points out, we would hesitate to make a distinction between 'a football match' and 'playing football' and yet that is what Langdon did between 'a play' and 'playing' – to most practitioners' approval. However, the theoretical language applied to drama today tends to reduce the distinction. Millward's phrase, for example, 'presenting experience dramatically' implies both process and product.

The concept of 'audience: a performing/experiencing dichotomy

To argue that there is in all classroom drama some sense of audience combined with some notion of performance is one thing, but to do this at the expense of ignoring key differences is another and here we begin to cry out for at least a sub category! One such will emerge in the following discussion.

An apparent dichotomy between what actors do and what children at play do was once more first mooted in England by the psychologist, James Sully (1896), who wrote 'A number of children playing at being Indians... do not 'perform' for one another. The words 'perform', 'act' and so forth all seem out of place here.' Harriet Finlay-Johnson rarely used the term 'performance', (although she did use 'acting') confining it to the rare occasion when her pupils gave a 'public performance'. Indeed she reiterates the point that she wants to 'do away with acting for display', which may seem at first sight to be an unconvincing protestation from someone whose pupils daily prepared (writing and rehearsing) plays for performing to the rest of the class. I believe, however, that **within Finlay-Johnson's expression 'acting for display' we have the seed of a major conceptual shift that will clear the way for a revised framework of classroom acting behaviour.**

I infer (and this is where I begin, necessarily, to reformulate *differences* in order to promote a truer understanding of audience as a common factor) that in banishing 'acting for display', Finlay-Johnson was attempting to remove from her pupils' acting behaviour that element that would normally have been seen as legitimate fodder for audience appraisal and appreciation – **the skill involved in the acting.** I noted above that she wanted to change the function of the audience, but she also wanted to change what they looked for: they were to give their attention to their fellow pupils' presentation as a medium for curriculum knowledge and avoid seeing it as an acting achievement to be applauded as such. Notice here that I have chosen the word 'presentation', not 'performance', for it did not seem appropriate to use the word 'performance' for an example of acting behaviour that sought to eliminate a proper attention given to **acting.** I want to suggest, therefore, **that the term 'performance', in a drama context, is most meaningful when it refers to acting for which an actor would expect to be applauded,** and that it be replaced by the term **'presentation' in respect of dramatic activity in which the acting is not highly relevant *in itself.*** In defining the terms in this way 'acting' and 'performing' are being used synonymously and '*performance*' may refer either to the acting retrospectively or to the occasion of the acting. Thus it follows that 'acting' or 'performing' is a *special sub-category* of that kind of acting behaviour one would expect of a 'presentation' (i.e. in which *showing* is the principal purpose).

It is this reordering of the basis for conceptual distinction that puts some of the activities of our pioneers in a different light. For instance, in respect of Finlay-Johnson, her intention to 'do away with display' places her work in the 'presentation' category – her pupils' endeavours at researching, script-writing and rehearsing are directed towards *presenting, not performing*. Caldwell Cook's work, on the other hand, unambiguously belongs to 'performing'. In other words, the principal purpose in *both* their classrooms is to *show*, but *additionally and significantly* in Caldwell Cook's classroom, the acting itself is up for approval as well as the content to be communicated. Thus 'performing', in this way of classifying, is not separate from presenting, but a special version of it.

Finlay-Johnson's pupils, according to these terms, were engaged in 'acting behaviour as a vehicle for curriculum knowledge'; Caldwell Cook's were 'acting' in its traditional or pure sense, in what Slade designated 'Acting in the full sense' – with a Capital 'A'. One fundamental effect of this change in rationale is that 'communication' can no longer be perceived as the prerogative of 'performing'. Other acting behaviours, involving some kind of 'presenting' (that is, depicting significant subject-matter for an audience to examine) require clear communication to an audience, but not their applause. It is conceivable, therefore, that the audience in part determines how the acting behaviour is to be perceived – what was intended by the players as a presentation could be turned by the audience into a performance. Just as Lars Kleberg (1993) argued that for an event to qualify as 'theatre', there must be present a spectator willing to see it '*as theatre*', so I am now suggesting that a spectator may also contribute to determining whether acting behaviour qualifies as 'performing' in its narrow or pure sense. The categories I am putting forward, 'performing' and 'presenting', are both concerned with conscious communication to an audience outside the drama. The extent to which skill of acting contributes to the meaning of that event, for actor or spectator, determines whether it belongs to 'presenting' or to its sub-category.

A further practical implication of this separation of 'performing', in a specific sense of being important in itself as an artistic skill, from other acting behaviours is that work by pupils on a script does not necessarily qualify the pupils' behaviour as '*performing*'. It is conceivable that while the performance of a play to another class or in school assembly or as a public performance is 'performing', the pupils' behaviour in the presentation of an excerpt from that same play as part of a classroom project on some social issue is not necessarily to be regarded as *performing* – unless, of course, the ethos of the school be such that pupils and teacher alike are conditioned to seeing enactment of any kind as demonstration of a skill awaiting applause. That is not to deny that there will be occasions within, for example, Process Drama when the artistry of the actors invites the expressed adulation of the spectators. This especially occurs in the final stage of the work when the students plan and rehearse a resolution of the story or issue, when the format being used is clearly of performance dimensions, *needing* the audience's approval of the performance as a performance for a sense of completion. Thus although I am making a conceptual distinction between 'performing' or 'acting in a pure sense' and other acting behaviours, this way of defining 'performing' by no means excludes it from the classroom. Indeed, training in stage acting might well be part of a course for upper adolescents in a secondary school specialising in the performing arts, in which case those students would necessarily concentrate their time within the 'performing' sub-division.

In the heading above, however, I have placed 'performing' and *'experiencing'* in polar opposition. There are, as we have seen, radical differences, to a point of mutual exclusion, between the performance behaviours, say, of Caldwell Cook's players and Millward's volcano-dwelling pupils, but 'experiencing' no longer seems the right choice of word for the culture-building at which the latter are working so hard. 'Experiencing' has a passive ring to it, but Millward's pupils are more than 'experiencing'; they are, as dramatists, forging a set of tacit laws within a cultural context; they are composing or constructing or, to give this kind of orientation a label, they are '**making**'. Such a category of acting behaviour (which in the past I have called 'dramatic playing', a term that nevertheless lacks the *active, composing* connotation of 'making') applies also to children's make-believe playing, to the kind of 'free' improvisations recommended in the 1960 textbooks such as 'be at the sea-side', to the sophisticated kind of tightly structured, small group exercises to be found in 'Process' Drama and to 'Mantle of the Expert' and all forms of 'living through'.

Thus I am suggesting the '**presenting**' classification, with its sub category, '**performing**' be set against a second category, '**making**'. It has sometimes been possible in the past to argue for 'performing' and 'experiencing' as alternative ends of a continuum, each with the potential for merging into the other, but the acting behaviour in 'making' taps everyday means of expression in order to signal the building, in 'now time', of a social or cultural entity and it could not logically 'merge into' either 'performing' or 'presenting' When Millward drew a distinction between 'presenting experience dramatically' and '*doing* Drama', he was alluding to a conceptual shift, not merely to a change of degree. 'Presenting'/'Performing' and 'Making' are indeed in a dichotomous relationship.

A further practical implication of this distinction is that an invitation in the classroom to '*do* drama' will commonly feed *performance* expectations, in which pupils, functioning as 'pupils', under a teacher's supervision, enact an improvised or scripted play. 'Go into your corners and make a up a play for us to see', will invariably invite 'performing', unless there is already in place an overriding interest in the topic. In 'living through drama' (or, 'making', as I am now labelling the acting behaviour) the children's function is not primarily mediated by their normal 'pupil/teacher' school role. They are 'makers' (dramatists) of 'life under a volcano'. Similarly the child playing at 'tractors' is not *primarily* functioning in a child/adult relationship, even if the mother is joining in the playing. The child's primary role is that of a dramatist, 'making' a 'tractor context'.

A Sense of Audience and Self-Spectator

If it can be agreed that all kinds of drama are potentially communicable to others outside the drama and that there is always at least an implicit product, then it is but a short step to further argue that a 'sense of audience' is properly present, whatever the methodology: if the pupil is 'performing', then s/he is subjecting herself/himself to an audience's appraisal, even if that audience is made up of just other members of the class or the teacher. If the child is 'making', whether in the sense of 'living through' under the guidance of a teacher-in-role or independent of an adult, then the pupil will be treating fellow pupils as audience in order jointly to present experience dramatically. If the drama is in the form of 'depiction' or 'tableau', or many of the other conventions now so popular in the classroom, then the demonstration is dependent on effective, accurate and economic signalling to a real or hypothetical audience. If the work is 'Mantle of the Expert', that special version of 'living through' drama, then the 'sense of audience', that is, a sense of who will need to understand what is being done to meet a contract, is paramount. This final example of 'audience', of course, resides in the participant himself, the 'self-spectator'. Emile Jacques-Dalcroze, writing in 1919 drew attention to the dual function of actor/spectator as follows: 'In the laboratory of his organism a transmutation is effected, turning the creator into both actor and spectator of his own composition'.

Hourd sees the adolescent's phase of development as one of uncomfortable, but temporary, self-awareness, she sees the pervasive purpose of enactment as a means of 'losing oneself to gain oneself' Taking this expression further, it seems that through the fiction one can, to use Bruce Wilshire's phrase 'come across oneself'. The fiction-making exposes the self reflected in it. It is as if the fiction is a mirror in which one might glimpse oneself. It is this view of 'self-spectatorship' Heathcote has absorbed into her work, while avoiding the therapeutic connotation that Hourd's expression 'losing oneself to gain one-self' could have. Heathcote's insistence on self-spectatorship is a deliberate harnessing of our capacity through Mimesis to examine our own values. She feels it is not something that can be left to chance.

Thus 'self-spectatorship', at its best, can be said to promote a double valence of being an audience to one's own creation and being an audience to *oneself*. Mike Fleming uses the term 'percipient' to combine the participant/spectator function in drama. Such a concept takes us beyond *individual* speculating to the *collective* feelings shared by all the players as 'an audience' to what they are creating or presenting. It further extends the theory of self-spectatorship to take on board the notion of the 'percipient's' emotional engagement with what is going on. The dimensions of 'playwright' and 'director' could also be added. The four functions, 'dramatist', 'spectator', 'participant' and 'director' are occurring simultaneously. This is so in *all* kinds of improvised drama, including children's informal play. Most of the past research into children's play has focused on the expressive components of a child's make believe be-haviour. Viewed from the perspective of a dramatist's or directorial functions, however, 'child-play' may be open to a new range of meanings, as evidenced by the research of Nelson and Seidman (1984), who see young children at play as making their own *scripts*.

The definition of acting behaviour may now be extended: **Acting behaviour is an act of fiction-making involving identification through action, the con-scious manipulation of time and space and a capacity for generalisation. It relies on some sense of audience, including self-spectatorship.**

Acting as a 'focus of responsibility'

Another dimension to a definition of drama resides in what could be des-cribed as the actor's 'burden of responsibility'. Even within broadly similar dramatic activities the focus of responsibility may be at variance. If we take, for example, Brian Way's methodology: in establishing that classroom drama was to be sans text, sans audience and sans acting, he was removing the tradi-tional responsibilities of an actor. Furthermore little importance was to be attached to *content*, so that his pupils were not to feel responsible even in that direction. He wanted them, however, to see what they were doing in terms of personal development and their prime attention was to be given to skills of concentration, sensitivity, intuition, speech and movement. I wish to argue here, therefore, that that particular orientation, the monitoring, largely to the exclusion of other elements, of how one is using one's personal skills, may be said to constitute, the acting behaviour of the participants. It could be said that, in this instance, the participant's make-believe behaviour is, at least in part, determined by his *intention* to privilege one kind of responsibility over another, to give attention to personal skills over content.

The idea of a 'defining orientation' in acting behaviour is perhaps more readily perceived in stage acting. Bert States (1985), for example, classifies acting into three modes, (self-expressive, collaborative and representational) as a way of describing the intention of an actor respectively to (1) display his skill to an audience, (2) relate to an audience or (3) demonstrate a play to an audience. States seems to be making the point that actors tend to favour (not exclusively, it should be said) one of these modal categories, involving an identifiable orientation, as part of an 'actor's presence'. States had a stage performance in mind, of course, but it is conceivable that such orientations could to some degree affect how, say, a small group of pupils show their prepared work to the rest of the class.

If we look at the process in a rehearsal room rather than on a stage, it is again possible to define the acting in terms of a different kind of intention or disposition. Two such contrasted imperatives are to be found in accounts of Stanislavski's rehearsals, for example. In the earlier stage of his well-docu-mented experimentation, he insisted on his actors being clear about a character's 'objectives' in order to justify each action; in his later career, how-ever, he encouraged his actors to plunge into action, letting the justification emerge from the physical. In these contrasted examples from Stanislavski, the kind of acting behaviour during rehearsal is dictated by the actors' choice, either to be disciplined by an intellectual impulse, or to be freed by a state of kinaesthetic receptivity. (Neither of these would apply, of course, if the actors or pupils were at the stage in rehearsal when lines should have been learned – their focal consciousness would be 'burdened' accordingly!)

Thus we have, from the above classroom, stage and rehearsal room, examples of three different kinds of factors determining the acting behaviour, which might be labelled as: *educational priorities, the actor's presence* and *the actor's way into a part*. The latter of course includes how the actor comes to *own* the 'givens' he is required to absorb.

Let us look further at how the classroom dictates the factors affecting the acting behaviour. Perhaps the clearest example may be drawn from Harriet Finlay-Johnson's 'shopping practice'. The overriding intention, as in all forms of acting, including stage and rehearsal room, is an agreement to 'play the drama game'; the defining feature of her pupils' acting behaviour is a simulation of what one does when one shops, including getting the arithmetic right. There may be something too, for some of the pupils, of States' self-expressive' mode: 'Look at me! I'm good at this!'. In Caldwell Cook's 'Mummery', how to translate Shakespeare's lines into an Elizabethan Playhouse design could be said to define the acting behaviour. For many teachers of English the acting of pupils engaged with Shakespearean texts would, by contrast, be described as 'making the meaning clear'.

It seems possible, then, to classify acting behaviour, according to the actor's focus of responsibility. We have already introduced this notion of 'responsibility' as the defining characteristic of acting in discussing Langdon's distinction between '*playing*' and '*a play*' when the added intention to communicate or entertain or please an audience *determines* the nature of the acting required of a 'play'. I suggest that to the extent that a participant consciously embraces one set of objectives over any alternatives, that commitment could be said to constitute his/her acting behaviour.

We may now put forward a conception of acting behaviour as a list of determining responsibilities.

1   distinguishing intention relating to content, character, dramatic form, self-spectator, performance skills and

2   where there is a formal or informal audience an expressive, communicative or demonstrative mode predominates and

3   extrinsic 'burdens', such as trying to remember lines, or a teacher-expectation, may further qualify or even dominate the acting behaviour.

Further determining responsibilities could be added relating specifically to Slade and Way's approach. We have already noted the 'temporal imperative' in their work where they use the fast action narration to accompanying actions by all the pupils together, and Way, we have earlier observed, created a new genre for the drama classroom: improvised drama as 'exercise', with all that entails of task-focused, short-term, practising or trying something out, or getting ready. Thus a fifth item of the above list of determinants would relate at times to a temporal imperative and/or to a limited expectation of the structure *per se*. At its worst, the latter 'exercise' form would invite an 'it's only an exercise' disposition. At its best, it could be seen as a tightly structured vehicle for honing in on some aspect of living in which the actor has committed interest. A dimension of responsibility thus can embrace the participant's attitude to the medium itself and to the understood purpose of doing the drama.

The actor's 'responsibilities' need to be seen as many-layered, variously relating to content, skill, style, audience, attitude and context. At times it would be appropriate to speak of 'intention' or 'disposition' or 'colour' or even, 'burden' as the defining metaphor, but I hope that my choice of 'focus of responsibilities' covers all these. This dimension should now be inserted into our definition above to read: **Acting behaviour is an act of fiction-making involving identification through action, a prioritising of determining responsibilities, the conscious manipulation of time and space and a capacity for generalisation. It relies on some sense of audience, including self-spectatorship.**

Summary

In this first section of the final chapter an attempt has been made gradually to build a definition of acting behaviours, a process of identifying the common ground or centre of its many forms. This involved a clarifying or even a reinterpreting of long-held concepts associated with classroom acting. The classification of the three major orientations of 'presenting', 'performing' (a subdivision of 'presenting') and 'making' made way for challenging past dichotomies bound up with the previously divisive notion of 'audience'. Acknowledging 'audience' as a common feature of acting behaviour, along with 'identification', 'manipulation of time and space', 'capacity for generalisation', and 'focus of responsibilities' amounts to a reformulation of theoretical positions. The most radical departure from traditional perception however may be ascribed to the notion underlying the classification into 'performing', and 'presenting', that 'acting' in its narrowest sense may be determined, not so much by identifiable behaviours, as by the combined intentions of the actors and audience.

Significantly, 'performing' has no place in 'making'. They represent two contrasted modes of acting behaviours. **On this premise is my reconceptualisation founded**. I am aware, however, that contemporary writers either fail to see a difference between them or do not regard such a difference as of importance in practice. In Ray Mather's excellent array of conventions, 'teacher-in-role', which I have claimed lures pupils into a particular form of 'making', is listed as but one of many conventions. This is fine for Mather's purpose which is to find images for helping his students acquire a language of theatre, but *teachers* I believe will work best if they are aware of the difference in power within each contrasted mode. To choose 'making' over 'presenting' or 'performing' or vice versa is to recognise the kind of experience each offers. It is with this in mind that I now want to clarify and summarise those features of 'making' that mark it as a unique form of acting behaviour. To achieve this it will be necessary **to rethink the very basis of 'living through' drama and child make-believe play.**

Characteristics of 'Making'

It seems from the above arguments that we can no longer characterise drama that is not specifically prepared for an audience as a 'self-expressive', 'personal', 'private', 'individual', and 'subjective' process – all the characteristics that used also to be thought to belong to child make-believe. Certainly both child play and 'living through' drama are examples of 'making', but I am proposing that the principal determinants are not to be found in the egocentric list in the above sentence but in directions that have not previously been considered. I will now list below the alternative criteria on which our classification of 'making', embracing 'living through' and child play, has been based.

Characteristics of 'Making', in respect of child play, some dramatic exercises, and 'living through' drama

1. Although there is an emphasis on 'process', a 'product' is being made to be reflected upon during or after the drama.
2. Each individual's contribution is part of a collective enterprise, culturally determined in language and action.
3. The activity is cultural in a second sense: the participants are creating their own make-believe identify with the underlying 'laws' of the social context being created. I believe this to be true of all child make-believe play. A child playing with dolls is examining the rules that belong to a mother/baby context. It remains egocentric to the extent that s/he is also seeking him/ herself within those rules – to see where s/he stands, as it were. S/he may be constructing the make-believe out of fear or power-seeking or wishful thinking, but it is the 'rules' of contextual behaviours s/he is exposing to herself. Likewise, in 'living through' drama, tacitly identifying the inner laws of whatever culture is being created is pre-eminent. This common link between make-believe play and 'living through' drama is, I believe, the key feature of both, but of course many

differences remain, including 'living through's' dependence on 'teacher-in-role'.

4. A third cultural feature is the kind of acting behaviours that 'making' re-quires. They are initially akin to the kind of common negotiating and affirming skills in language and non verbal communication required of people involved in establishing any social event in 'real life'. They re-inforce a strong sense of 'it is happening now; we are making it happen; we are watching it happen'. But because of this existential sense of it *occurring* now, it is not repeatable and because of the initial dependence on a *collective* effort, the normal entry into dramatic fiction of pursuing an individual *character* is not so readily available. It may not be *repeatable* but in 'living through' drama it is *interruptible* and *episodical* – a good teacher will recognise when a plateau, dead end or crossroads has been reached and know that it is necessary temporarily to come out of the fiction in order to go back in again at an enhanced level.

5. A fourth sense in which the activity is cultural relates to who the parti-cipants see themselves as before they start their drama-making. If they are friends in a garden their identity, including past history as friends, determines how they enter the make-believe. If they are pupils in a school invited to 'make up a play', *who* they are is unequivocally determined by that teacher/pupil context. If, however, they are led into 'living through' drama by a teacher in role, the parameters of their role as pupils and their teacher's role as 'teacher' *slacken*. There is a sub-cultural shift, unique to 'living through' drama, easing them into the fictitious context.

6. There is a related *aesthetic* dimension. In the normal '*doing* drama', there are a number of 'givens' – ideas, information, a plan, characters, their own or someone else's script or even a teacher's instructions. These givens exist in a medium of their own – pictures, memories, ideas, images, words on paper or words spoken etc., and the task is to translate them into dramatic form, what Schechner calls the raw food waiting to be cooked by art. In 'living through' drama the givens, provided by the teacher in role are already expressed in the medium of dramatic art (partially cooked) so that no bridging is required of the pupils from one medium to another.

7. The teacher in role provides a challenging model of belief, style and dramatist's skills, so that in every aspect of the art the participant (*inside* the dramatic event) is invited to reach beyond his/her present com-petence and to acquire an understanding of how theatre works at a deeper level than if s/he were *outside* 'doing drama'.

8. The scope for manipulating time and space is limitless and fluid providing it is meaningful to the other players.

9. The *responsibility* of each participant is that of a dramatist/actor/director/spectator. It is a multi artistic function. When a child enters make-believe s/he is remaking her known world (in so far as she is looking at 'what the rules are' of that known world] by trying out a dialogue, trying out a plot, trying out actions etc. that reflect those rules – and observing herself in all that. The *pretending* or *impersonating* is but one aspect of these multi-responsibilities. Much observation of child play I believe suffered from focusing merely on the pretending. The actor on stage, of course, does not have these extended responsibilities.

10. A quality that 'making' shares with 'stage acting' is what Frost and Yarrow (1990) name disponibilité: 'It's a kind of total awareness, a sense of being at one with the context: script, if such there be, actors, audience, theatre space, oneself and one's body (p152)'.

It is the combination of the above ten features that leads us to insist on seeing 'making' as a special category of acting behaviour, especially when a 'living through', that is, a 'teacher-in-role-led' approach to drama is adopted. Our category table could now look like this:

classroom acting behaviours

| presenting | making | performing |

'Presenting' includes acting behaviours in a wide range of activities, such as tableau, depiction, sculpting, acting from a script, forum theatre, chamber theatre etc. – any of the forms of acting where the responsibility to 'show' has priority. It is rehearsable and repeatable. 'Making' includes the acting behaviours of children's make-believe playing, 'living through' drama, 'hot-seating' and the kind of acting in any dramatic exercise in which the participants are free to explore without any sense of preparing for showing to someone else. It is not rehearsable nor directly repeatable. **I should perhaps reiterate the warning that this classification of acting behaviour as 'making' should not be confused with Hornbrook's categorisation of 'making' and 'performing' as but two stages in a dramatic process.**

Is *theatre* a feature common to 'making' and 'presenting'?

Perhaps the crudest definition of theatre is Eric Bentley's (1975:150) 'A impersonates B for C'. Bruce Wilshire (1982) elaborates on this, pointing out that the Greek word for theatre (*theotron*, a place for seeing) is linked with *theoria* which can both mean spectacle and speculation or theory. 'Thus', concludes

Wilshire, 'it is suggested that theatre, at its origins, was its own mode of speculating and theorising about human nature and action (p33)'. Such a definition, Wilshire admits, takes the wonder out of theatre until one appreciates that *theoria* can also mean 'to look god in the face'. It is towards the mystery of theatre that Peter Brook (1993) turns. He defines theatre in the following terms. 'The essence of theatre is within a mystery called 'the present moment' (p81). He later extends it into a mysticism that would have appealed to Peter Slade:

> It (theatre) is the truth of the present moment that counts, the absolute sense of conviction that can only appear when a unity binds performer and audience. This appears when the temporary forms have served their purpose and have brought us into this single, unrepeatable instant when a door opens and our vision is transformed. (p96)

Thus theorists of theatre appear to swing between the functional and the poetic. Ken Robinson (1980), for instance, sees theatre as a kind of social encounter between actors and audience; '...it is partly their presence (the audience) and their activity which identifies what is going on as theatre.' By comparison, for Peter Slade, theatre is 'a golden moment' He writes: 'I felt the light dying. If not of the real sun, it was the light of 'real theatre' when a great scene comes to a close.' It seems that the place where an encounter can occur between audience and actors may be called 'a theatre' and that, more importantly, the encounter itself is to be called 'theatre'. Sometimes, however, 'theatre' is used as a criterion of effectiveness – Fleming (1994) refers to Heathcote's 'Three Looms Waiting' as qualifying for the description of 'an effective piece of theatre'. From Brook and Slade we see that special moments of ecstasy are to be called 'theatre'. In describing 'Process Drama' Cecily O'Neill (1995) uses the contemporary language of theatre; her conclusion about a completed Process Drama experience is that: 'The experience was its own destination and the group an audience to its own acts.' In my 1979 publication *Towards a Theory of Drama Education* I wrote, misleadingly I now believe, of theatre as being one of three broad kinds of dramatic activity to be promoted in schools: 'theatre' (meaning 'performing to an audience'), 'dramatic playing' (meaning improvisational and without an audience), and 'exercise' (meaning 'practising something'). Then, perhaps more usefully, in the same book, I introduced the idea of 'theatre form', referring to such elements as 'tension', 'focus', 'surprise', 'contrast' and 'symbolisation'. For Heathcote, as we have seen, theatre '...has many 'communicating faces' that surround and give variety of shapings to a few operant laws'. Its dimensions are 'movement/stillness', 'sound/silence', and 'light/darkness'.

I am reluctant to deny any of the above usages. It may be that in discussing formal elements it is more useful, as Hornbrook (1989) does, to employ the term 'dramatic art', in which case the most common usage of 'theatre' could be left to a combination of place and occasion when actors perform to an audience. And yet to see Process Drama, a sequence dependent on a mixture of 'making' and 'presenting' as a new genre of *theatre* has its attractions. Perhaps it is the *overall* experience that qualifies for the name, leaving particular components of the sequence to be rated as *dramatic art*. I suspect that common usage will continue to use these terms loosely. I certainly have no conclusive feelings on the matter.

Conclusion

Let us now reconsider some of the positions briefly outlined in the Introduction to this book in the light of the historical account attempted in these eleven chapters and of some of the conclusions I have come to in this chapter. I began by quoting John Allen who argued that 'drama in schools is basically and essentially no different from drama anywhere else.' Out of the context of his 1979 publication this seems to be no more than a platitude. One cannot disagree with it, but does it mean anything useful? The answer, of course, is that it *did* at the time of his writing when the very language of drama teachers became exclusive, divisive and sectarian. Allen was responding to a philosophical schism that separated drama into public/private, audience-centred/childcentred, product/process, performing/experiencing, and theatre/play dichotomies. The model I have presented here serves, I hope, to break up these dualities. Of particular importance is my conclusion that all kinds of acting behaviours rely on a sense of audience.

If we turn, however, to the quotation cited in the Introduction from David Hornbrook, who claimed 'that conceptually there is nothing which differentiates the child acting in the classroom from the actor on the stage in the theatre', we will see that my model puts forward an alternative position without seeking to defend the kind of thinking about performing that led Hornbrook to make his rather extreme statement. I am suggesting that performing *per se* is defined by the interest of the actors and/or spectators. This is acting (I am using 'acting' and 'performing' synonymously) in its purest or most traditional sense, applying equally to what the actor does on stage and to what the child *may do* in the classroom. Differences in such features as quality, style, or spontaneity will vary from classroom to classroom and from stage to stage, but essentially it qualifies as 'performing' because it commands attention to itself as an achievement.

'Presenting' may or may not focus on 'performing'. The players and audience may be emotionally engaged by the material illustrated; it may qualify as 'dramatic art', but if for both the audience and the players *what* is being said excludes for a particular audience how it is being said, making applause for 'the performance' redundant, then it fulfils solely a presentational function. Of course, the spectators may spontaneously applaud their approval of the 'message', as one would applaud a speaker at a meeting, without giving undue attention to it as a performance. Clearly in practice the two forms of 'performance' and 'presentation' may be so fluid that which applies in relation to any particular piece of work could remain academic. In the educational context of a classroom it is not so important in itself always to be able to draw a clear distinction between the two as it is to recognise that in an educational setting there may be times when an inappropriate degree of attention is directed towards performing skills. Of course the School's sub-cultural context will often control how a piece of work may be seen. In responding to the *same* stimulus, a Theatre Studies class may automatically rely on a 'performance' frame of mind whereas a 'presentation' of the same piece would more likely satisfy a Social Studies class.

'Making' as a category of acting behaviour (not to be confused with Hornbrook's usage of the term) is unlikely to be treated as other than what it is, a form of behaviour distinctly different from 'presenting' and 'performing'. Its ten characteristics listed above are an indication of how complex it can be, especially in its 'living through' version. It represents a hugely important educational and dramatic tool. To ignore 'living through' drama, as some recent publications appear to do, is to deprive our pupils of a firm basis for understanding dramatic art. It is not enough to recommend 'improvisation', for much improvisation is mostly performance oriented. The ideal teacher uses the strengths of 'presenting' (including 'performing') *and* 'making'. In Mike Fleming's latest publication he shows teachers how approaches to texts can embrace a wide range of tableaux, depiction, games, script work, 'living through' drama, dramatic exercises, and 'hot-seating' (Fleming, 1997).

I hope that the framework I am recommending allows for an eclectic approach. It may perhaps be most vividly illustrated by reference to the many versions of the ever popular 'blindfold' exercise recorded earlier. At one extreme we have Clive Barker's acting exercise from Peking Opera in which acting technique alone is required to convey being blindfolded (other examples include Brian Way's and Constantin Stanislavski's sense deprivation exercises 'to find out what it is like to be blind' and Cecily O'Neill's 'hunter and hunted' game as a means of reviving, after a break, the atmosphere of the

'Frank Miller' drama) and, at the opposite extreme we have Peter Millward's nine year olds play-making in which they subtly create blindness in a character by the way they treat him: 'Ah, here he is now... Come on... careful... over here... come on... mind the steps... Right... he made it.' This latter may be seen as a perfect example of 'making' in that it illustrates the *dramatist* function, even in relatively young children; Clive Barker's may be seen as a 'pure' example of acting technique. I hope the framework caters for both these extremes and for the other examples too.

That fiction-making is at the centre of all the activities appears to support the educational advocacy that drama provides a creative way of looking at the world. In this respect I believe Edmond Holmes, writing in 1911, was wise to see drama as having a rather different function from the other arts, but that is a matter for others to look into. Holmes wrote of dramatisation as '...teaching them to identify themselves, if only for a moment, with other human beings' He claimed this demonstrated the 'sympathetic' function of drama as an educational tool. This may be to err in the direction of a degree of 'compassion' which I do not believe drama necessarily feeds. Nevertheless, Holmes seems to be feeling towards the recognition that drama promotes some kind of relationship between the 'self' and 'the world'. Of growing importance in the vocabulary of writers in recent years is the notion of 'self-spectator', a conception that enactment leads to seeing oneself reflected in the fiction one is making. I have argued for 'fiction-making' as the defining nucleus for all acting behaviours. Perhaps 'self-spectatorship' should be regarded as the definitive outcome.

Aims and Objectives

In recent years there has been a pressure to produce attainment targets in drama leading to a tendency to look for skills based objectives dealing with handling drama form. This is chapter 6 from *New perspectives on classroom drama* (1992). Bolton provides a useful antidote to this focus on form by insisting that form and content cannot be separated. It offers a concise guide to the drama teacher sorting out his or her goals in drama teaching.

The history of Drama Education in England (in Bolton, 1984) tells a pendulum-swinging story. From the early days of text-centred drama of the Speech and Drama teachers, to the headier days of the child-centred approach of Peter Slade (1954), and from the content-centred work of Dorothy Heathcote, to the skill-centred approach of some current writers, trends often borne of political pressures which have pushed teachers in contrary directions.

I think it is useful here to attempt to categorise the aims that have been variously followed by past practitioners. In spite of the wide philosophical divergences, it is possible to detect but four main aims that all drama teachers at all times have tended to maintain. There have been those who:

1. place an emphasis on content;
2. promote drama for personal growth;
3. see drama principally as a means of social development;
4. hold teaching about the dramatic art form as a priority.

In several recent articles (1989, 1990) I attempted to elaborate on these categories. I claimed that the good Drama teacher attempts to move forward on all of these fronts simultaneously, sometimes, because of the nature of the work or the nature of the class, giving more attention to one than the other.

When it came to expanding on Category 4 I found myself at odds with some current writers, including those of official DES (1984, 1989, 1990) and NCC (1990) documents. They almost totally ignore dimensions of form which, as shown in earlier chapters, provide the basis for my theory and practice of Drama Education. I am referring to concepts such as focus and tension, which are created by the deliberate manipulation of time and space, and by the imposition of constraints. These critical formal dimensions are given little space in recent literature, almost as though those now writing about drama theory do not really understand the basic nature of drama.

The trap in attempting to categorise lies in the very separation of concepts that should not be isolated. In recent writings I have divided Category 4 into four subcategories:

a) Learning how to act;
b) Academic learning about drama;
c) Learning theatre crafts;
d) Learning the basic elements of drama.

But I have been so alienated by the dualism apparent in the The Arts 5-16 project, in which the writers promote the erroneous notions of Education *through* the Arts and Education *in* the Arts, that I have felt compelled to take Subcategory d from category 4 in order to join it up with Category 1. Hence the concept of 'content/form', which I hope will re-establish in teachers' minds that when you are working in one of the Arts, you are drawing on the interdependence of the two. Category 4, losing its critical 'basic elements' to

Aims in drama teaching

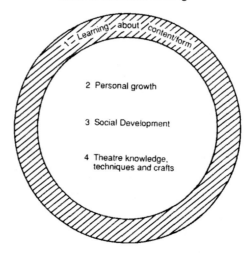

Category 1, can now be described as 'Theatre knowledge, Techniques and Crafts'. Diagramatically, the four categories can be expressed as shown in the figure (opposite).

Learning about content/form

Most writers in the Arts, even those that seek to promote a separation between Education *through* the Arts and Education *in* the Arts, agree that the Arts are concerned with bringing about some new understanding. I quote from the document *The Arts 5-16* (NCC, 1990):

> 'The arts ... are concerned with many different ways of knowing the world...' (p26 A Curriculum Framework)

> 'The arts ... are concerned not only with what we perceive in the world but with the *qualities* of human perceptions; with how we experience the world.' (*ibid.*)

> 'They may also be creative in the more profound sense of generating new ways of seeing.' (p27 A Curriculum Framework)

> '... at some times the artist is an iconoclast who challenges prevailing attitudes and values; at others, artists are 'the voice of the community', shaping images and artifacts to give form to a community's deepest values and convictions.' (*ibid.*)

All of the above quotes give support to the idea that the Arts are to do with understanding the world anew, in respect of the qualities of our perceptions and the values we bring to bear on what we perceive. Drama teachers, perhaps more than other Arts teachers, have tended in the last 20 years or so to articulate the purpose of their work in these kinds of terms. Although such statements may be true of other Art forms – certainly it is apparent in all written forms of Art – it is easier for Drama teachers and playwrights to see their work being aimed at engaging directly with the world, for Drama relies on the world for its material. If you like, 'the world' is the dramatist's *curriculum*. But as I have said in Chapter 3 (p36), it is not the playwright's job to describe the world in a *factual* sense, but in a *truthful* sense. The playwright illuminates some kind of truth about the world (which, of course, includes ourselves), and s/he achieves this through the use of *form*. The 'content' of a play is 'content-as-illuminated-by-form', and the emerging truth is born of that content/form particularity. Of course, for the sake of convenience in dealing with it we, as an audience or as academics, may generalise from it. This is a reductionist process which is always in danger of denying the original experience, like contenting ourselves with labelling Shakespeare's *Othello* as being about 'jealousy'. Unavoidably, the moment we attempt to reflect on how an art product might have significance for us, we move away from its particularity. There is an interaction occurring between the particular that is the play and the particular that is *me*, and if, further, I want to share my response with someone else, I will no doubt be driven to finding a sufficient level of generalisation to afford communication.

The interdependence of content/form has implications for the teacher and pupils in the classroom. The world is also *their* curriculum, to be illuminated by dramatic form. In this respect the teacher and students in the classroom are not doing anything different from what playwrights, directors and actors are trying to achieve. To say that it is possible, as *The Arts 5-16* project claims, to use drama as a method of relating to content in some way that is different from the kind of drama one uses in 'making drama' is absurd, for any 'making drama' must be about some significant content.

There is a form of dramatic usage in schools, often referred to as Simulation or Role-play for skill training, that has little to do with dramatic art, where children take on roles in order to assimilate facts or develop behavioural skills. Although it may well carry the 'imperative tension' of something important happening, what in fact often happens is that everyone's attention is focused on the skill of the participant: 'Is s/he handling the simulated interview adequately?' ... 'Is s/he conducting this simulated counselling sensitively?' ... 'Does s/he (the trainee doctor) answer the patient's (simulated) questions?' ... 'Does s/he bring the management team to a reasonable point of agreement?' ... 'Given the alternatives, does s/he arrive at a sensible decision?' ... 'Does s/he get rattled as we pile on the pressures – in this (of course) fictitious situation?'. Such activities are to drama as diagrams are to visual art – they are denotative rather than connotative. There is no protection either by the fiction (for in this case the supposed fiction replicates the pressures of 'real life' too closely) or by the character; indeed it is one's own personality that is being tested.

Surely the NCC publication, *The Arts 5-16*, cannot be advocating a balanced diet between 'diagrams' and 'paintings', between Simulation and Drama as an art form? I think it more likely that the writers of the project do not understand that *Drama is always about something*. Inescapably, there are always content, theme, substance, subject matter and curriculum. There is no such thing as a division between Education *in* and Education *through* the Arts. Even the simplest form of drama with kindergarten children must be using the art form to illuminate some truth about the world; otherwise dramatic activity simply remains at the 'diagram' level of reiterating facts or practising skills. Let me make it clear that I am not *against* Role-play or Simulation. They have their place in education and training, and, indeed, Drama teachers from time to time may employ such exercises as part of a cumulative sequence. But our overriding aim is always to achieve *understanding* through the art form.

Sometimes you are aware that your work has slipped into something that amounts to no more than Simulation. I have occasionally come across Drama teachers who set up a kind of drama that is little different from a 'discussion'. (I have done it myself in off moments!) I call this kind of work 'Swimming Pool' drama. I have taken the title from those lessons where the teacher poses a problem: 'You are members of the town council. You have one million pounds left over. Do you want to spend it on a swimming pool or a home for the elderly?'. There is little chance of 'ownership' of these roles. There is also little chance of finding an interesting use of, for example, focus or constraint to give the experience form. This is a kind of dramatised discussion, *which may still have educational value but it is not dramatic art.* Here I shall give an example from my own practice of what I mean by dramatic art.

Some time ago I was asked to teach Road Safety to a class of six-year olds. If I had wanted to *avoid* drama I could have set up a simulation exercise, where-by the children had the chance to practise road drill: looking right, left and then right again before crossing an imaginary road. This would amount to Simulation practice – 'drawing diagrams'. But as it was *drama* I wanted to use, I set up a fictitious situation where we invented a five-year old boy called Michael. On his birthday he rushed home from school instead of waiting for his parent and was knocked down by a car. We did *not* simulate the accident. I decided that I should be 'in role' as Michael's parent and the class as Michael's neighbours. What we experienced was the parent arriving home, thinking that Michael must surely have got home first and was hiding: 'Michael? ... Michael, I know you're hiding ...', I called, at first in fun and then, as the silence followed each call, more and more desperately. Then I included the neighbours by asking them whether they had seen him – perhaps he was hiding in their homes. Then, on the neighbours' advice, I decided to phone the school, but I was too worried to make the call: 'Could one of you ...?', and so on. Eventually we learnt there had been an accident and that Michael was in hospital. He had run across a road without looking first.

For me this is working *in* the art form. What we experienced was that moment when a name was called, and there was no answer. The silence was awesome. I believe that it was this silence that took us, the children and me together, close to realising what ignoring the road-safety rules can *amount to.* It also gave some point to learning the Road Safety Code.

To ask of my lesson, 'Was it Education *through* the Arts or Education *in* the Arts?' is totally absurd. As far as I was concerned we were working in the art form using elements of theatre, and we had a firm grasp of the kind of content we were setting out to explore. As a teacher I was observing their understanding of the theme, and whether they could extend the theatrical context I had started: to what extent, for instance, were the children able to enjoy the *withholding* of the news about the accident, so that the tension of not knowing could be fully experienced?; to what extent could they 'pick up' the effectiveness of the counterpoint between the calling and the silence? Notice too the obliqueness of the focus chosen by the teacher to open up this area of knowledge. This is not using drama as a *method*, although the writers of *The Arts 5-16* appear to think it is.

I will give an example from Secondary teaching, again to make my point about choosing material that happened to be in someone's syllabus – this time History. The History textbook included a kind of 'dramatic' activity that was 'diagram drawing' at its worst. The authors, in their chapter on the American War of Independence, included something that looked like a play-script. The rift between the people of New York and the British Government was expressed through the mouths of the owner of a New York coffee house and a well-known customer visiting from London. Each character's dialogue stated the opposing arguments in a way that was meant to help the students remember the relevant viewpoints. This is an example of Simulation, the equivalent of practising Road Safety. The students would no doubt remember the relevant facts as a result of this dramatic technique, *but it is not drama*. I asked my class to become scriptwriters and to turn the text they had in front of them in their History books into 'real' drama. 'How do you speak to your customers when you are setting up a business? ... Suppose that customer riles you with his erroneous political views? ...', and the class began to realise the meaning of *subtext*: it is the *constraint* on the owner of the coffee shop that makes drama; it is the things that are *not* said that matter. The paradox of working in the art form of drama in this way is that, like the silence when Michael did not answer (see above), we are drawn nearer to the meaning of what is going on because it remains implicit. Again, it becomes nonsense to ask whether we were working *through* the Arts or *in* the Arts.

Form

I hope the above examples also make clear the interdependence of content/ form. In Chapters 2 and 3 I drew attention to the basic components of theatre form (not to be confused, as some recent writers are guilty of doing, with theatre conventions or genres). Some of them are listed below as a reminder:

- *Focus or Imperative tension* provides the dynamic for dramatic form: our attention is engaged by something that must happen
- *Tension* through the manipulation of time and space
- *Tension* through the imposition of 'constraints', that is the withholding of true facts, true feelings, true wants
- *Ritual*
- *Temporary chaos*, through the *breaking* of constraint or ritual

There is a cluster of theatrical concepts which form part of tension and ritual: *deception; seeming; magic; order; disorder; power; ambiguity; harmony, contrast,* etc. Each is part of the excitement of theatre. It is the teacher's responsibility, no matter how young the children are, to foster a sense of theatre which they may or may not be able to articulate. Suppose in the Road Safety lesson above, some of the children were not able to 'withhold' their superior knowledge that Michael had had an accident. I would have had a number of choices: I could have stopped the drama and invited them to 'see what it's like to watch Michael's father calling a child because he does not know what has happened'; when the experience was over I could have talked about whether 'we could have made it more exciting if we had not told Michael's father straightaway'; I could have borne in mind that, the next time I did drama with this class, I would test them with a similar situation where the constraint of withholding the truth for the sake of the drama was again demanded of them. This simple knowledge of the 'game of theatre' is something that Drama classes must understand and appreciate as soon as possible, and teachers should continually be alert to opportunities for teaching that game.

Just as I am critical of the writers of *The Arts 5-16* for encouraging Drama specialists to feel that they can teach their art without respect for content, so I am equally critical of those teachers who give little attention to the need to improve their pupils' ability to handle the art. About two years ago I sat in at a session of a course for teachers from an outer London borough. The tutor asked the class of teachers to write down and classify their aims in teaching Drama. There was a long list dealing with subject matter, and personal and social development, but not one teacher put forward 'improvement in doing drama' as an aim. Indeed, when I suggested that they had missed out this vital aim, there was a slightly shocked response as though I had committed some professional gaffe.

Content

In the theatre and in the classroom, drama is a way into knowledge: it opens up new ways of looking at things. Through theatrical metaphor the world we live in is explored. But while it is possible to *indicate* the door that is being opened by the play or the classroom drama sequence, one cannot specify what any one individual will learn, or even guarantee that s/he will go through that door! Just as one cannot in any absolute sense explain what an art product is about other than in terms of itself, so one cannot identify what a particular person will learn. We can only *indicate* what something is about and *indicate* what we think someone has learnt.

The teacher may be able to plan in broad terms using the notion of learning *area*, but because it is art the teacher is not in a position to be more explicit. I like the concept of 'opening a door'. The Maths teacher, or even the History teacher (the kind who goes for facts, that is), may find it easy to be specific. Indeed, much Simulation-type dramatic method will allow for explicitness. In the Road Safety example above, no doubt the 'practice road drill' simulation would lead to a checklist haven for those teachers who see the exercise as one of learning to 'look right, then left, etc'. But how could I, in the lesson I actually conducted, know *precisely* either what I intended the children to learn or, after the event, what they did learn? All I can know is that 'a door may have been opened' to an understanding of what failing to keep the Road Safety Code *amounts to*. In talking to the children afterwards, observing their pictures or written accounts, hearing what they tell their parents, or noting their change in attitude towards Road Safety, one might glean what has been understood. But such an emerging picture needs time. Something during the drama, immediately after it, the next day, the next week, or the next term may show itself; or what has been learnt may not be revealed at all. In some cases nothing may have worked for a particular child.

Nevertheless, one persists in trying at least to identify the 'door'. In working with a group of lower adolescents on the topic of cancer I chose the theme of two kinds of 'caring': the professional caring of doctors and nurses and the kind of caring expressed by the family when someone suffers from cancer. I chose this angle as a 'learning area'. I could not foresee what each individual in the class would make of my deliberate juxtaposition within the drama sequence of these two kinds of caring – sometimes the participants were 'in role' as medical staff, at other times as parents of a patient – but I believe there is a greater chance of a door being opened and of the class going through when the teacher knows at least which door it is.

In using the term 'learning area', you should be aware of its limitations. Just as someone does not go to the theatre intent to learn something, weighed down by something called a 'learning area', so in the classroom the learning that goes on is indirect. A participant's focus of attention is primarily on creating an art product (through illustrative/performance activity)[1] or creating a fictitious social context (through dramatic playing). Learning occurs at a level of, to use Polanyi's (1958) useful term, 'subsidiary awareness'.

Thus dramatic activity is always, albeit obliquely, related to knowledge. I have already asserted that this is not the explicit knowledge of skills and facts, but that kind of knowledge related to values, principles, implications and responsibility – what skills and facts *amount to*. The distinction is probably easier to grasp if we talk in terms of 'understanding' rather than 'knowledge'. So often the school context can only think of knowledge in terms of propositional knowledge: a verbal statement about a fact. For instance most six-year olds '*know*' that careless attention to the Road Safety Code can lead to an accident, but this is not to *understand* it. The understanding can only come from direct experience, or from the mediated experience of an art form, one medium being drama.

One problem for the teacher is that this kind of learning is as intangible as it is significant and, as I have intimated above (see above), can take some considerable time to reveal itself. Another problem is what such learning should be called. 'Conceptual' seems to be the most appropriate, but this is often associated with a purely intellectual process. However, I cannot think of anything better, so 'conceptual' will have to do, provided we acknowledge that feelings are engaged in the development of concepts.

Mental skills
Accompanying conceptual learning are a number of mental skills that drama activity continually draws on. The very act of make believe is a mental activity in that:

- it requires an 'as if' frame of mind;
- it requires the motivation and the ability to sustain the 'as if';
- it encourages hypothesis before a fictitious event – 'What would happen if. ..?', we ask ourselves;
- it encourages 'reading between the lines' of what is being expressed, particularly as we have seen in 'illustrative' work;
- it encourages the anticipation of consequences;

- it requires both the recognition of the logic controlling a social event and the application of that logic to it;
- it encourages weighing up the pros and cons in decision-making;
- it encourages looking at implications after an event;
- it encourages sifting out the values implicit within an action;
- it encourages honest reflection on an event, the careful selection of what should be recorded and *how*, using forms as varied as recalling 'feelings' to categorising 'findings';
- above all it develops the capacity for 'standing outside oneself', seeing one's actions, thoughts and experiences as 'objects' to be reflected upon.

The Russian psychologist, Luria (1959), wrote of two sisters he observed in their play, selecting to play 'at being twins'. It is often assumed that *absorption* is a key feature of dramatic activity but, in fact, *detachment* is of equal importance. This is what Dorothy Heathcote refers to as 'decentring'. It is a double featured process:

- detaching oneself from the content in order to examine it and learn from it;
- detaching oneself from the *theatre form* in order to examine *how* something was achieved.

These are equally important processes in the promotion of learning. Now I shall look at other aims, distinguishable from but not independent of content/form.

Personal growth

For many teachers in the 1950s and 1960s in England, Personal Development was seen as having priority over all other aims. In a sense, of course, education must finally be concerned with development of the person. That being so, we are all advocates of personal development. But, obviously, the pioneers of Personal Development as a philosophy for Drama Education intended a special usage of the term. Their emphasis was on self-expression, personal identity, self-esteem, sensitivity, the 'uniqueness of the individual', and on the maturing process. Such a philosophy was part of the progressive movement in education but, like all forms of emphasis, it can only be fully understood in terms of what it was countering. In Drama Education, English pioneers, such as Peter Slade (1954) and Brian Way (1967), were putting forward alternative views of the child, of education and of drama. This was in reaction to the rigid perception of the child as an empty vessel, education as rote learning and drama as stage performance. Again, like all forms of emphasis, while in the early days there has to be an overstatement of the case in order to attract attention, subsequently such an emphasis outlives its usefulness as its message becomes absorbed by the general educational movement.

It is the *emphasis* that becomes anachronistic, not the truth it promotes. A new emphasis does not necessarily deny the value of its predecessor. Such is the case here. It is clear from the earlier diagram that I am posing *Content/ form* as superseding the other three categories, each of which has, at one time or another, claimed prior attention over the others. But that is not to disregard the important role that Personal Growth, Social Development, and Theatre Knowledge, Techniques and Crafts play in Drama Education. Promoters of Personal Development as a philosophy were concerned to identify the affective dimension in the learning process. I hope that the Road Safety lesson [described earlier], for example, demonstrates how the content/ form objective is achieved through a feeling/thinking dramatic process. It is the affective component that puts the participant in touch with the significance of things.

It may be that, with the current regrettable political interference in education, we will need to return to re-emphasising Personal Development, especially in relation to such qualities as independence of mind, curiosity, initiative, self-criticism and responsibility. Just this morning on the radio (November 14, 1990) a past Education Minister and headmaster, Sir Rhodes Boyson, and his colleague launched an appeal for raising standards in Education. When his colleague exclaimed, 'We need to teach the three Rs', Sir Rhodes Boyson added, 'Of course, Education is about more than the three Rs'. I gave three cheers and anticipated that he was perhaps going to talk about values, developing the whole person, etc., but he continued, 'Education is also vocational and technical!

Generally speaking, Personal Development and its associated skills of expression related to language and movement can be seen as an ongoing aim, whatever the more explicit content/form aim may be. In this sense one is *always* promoting self-esteem, creating opportunities for experimentation in expression, putting participants in touch with their feelings, etc. These might be called 'soft' objectives, as opposed to the 'hard' objectives of content/form in relation to a *specific* piece of work. Nevertheless, there are times when Personal Development, especially in responding to evident special needs of an individual, is uppermost in the teacher's mind and takes priority over content/form objectives, for instance: making sure the shy child has the chance to articulate his/her ideas; throwing out a challenge to the glib child; building the stature of the ignored child; drawing in the sceptical child; providing an opening for the unsure child to take the initiative. At such times, of course, teacher-in-role is indispensable, for this kind of delicate handling can usually only be managed from 'inside' the creative process. It is not something that the teacher can attend to with any degree of subtlety from the 'touch-line'. On such occasions, and they are fairly common, content/form objectives may be held in abeyance. It does not matter a bit whether or not the child has a grasp on the central concept; that the drama has created an opportunity for self-advance-ment is all that is important.

There is a sense in which all conceptual knowledge is bound up with self. Whereas pioneers such as Brian Way (1967) saw Drama Education as directly developing self-awareness, my preference is to see such growth in terms of the 'self' being affected reflexively by the content/form, that is, in the process of engaging formally with a theme one is brought face-to-face with oneself. It is as if the content/form provides the mirror in which we see ourselves. This is brought home no more forcibly than when watching a comedy in the theatre: the audience's laughter is that of *recognition.*

There is another sense in which 'self' plays a major part in what is being created. I am referring to *self-commitment.* I sometimes say to my classes, 'You cannot do drama unless you 'give a little bit of yourself' to it'. To em-phasise this with young adults I will sometimes start a workshop that gives them the chance to share something personal about themselves with the rest of us, and to present the information dramatically. This approach invites them to take a personal risk right at the beginning of the work. I am not recommending to the reader that s/he should rush to his/her classes with this kind of activity in mind – its suitability needs to be carefully judged.

[...]

Social development

It is not surprising that disciples of the humanist movement in the 1960s and 1970s saw drama as a key strategy for social development. The popularity of 'encounter groups', 'T groups', 'Gestalt group-therapy', etc., stemming from the theoretical work and practice of Rogers (1961), Perls (1969) and Maslow (1954), focused attention on group interaction as a key factor in the maturing process. Drama, essentially an ensemble process, was ripe for plucking. Many teachers, influenced by this movement, started to view drama work solely in terms of *group* behaviour, with special emphasis on group *autonomy.*

I can recall many years ago hearing from a frustrated participant who had attended a weekend Drama course for teachers. The course was conducted by a friend of mine who, believing absolutely in the value of group autonomy, had left the group for the whole weekend to decide 'what they wanted to do'. They never found out! In my earliest days of using the device of 'What do you want to make a play about?', I think I deceived myself into thinking I was following the 'new' humanist philosophy. My *real* reason was that it is very difficult to impose content/form on a group you have never met before. As I was, due to the nature of my job, continually meeting fresh groups, I allowed confusion to grow in the minds of teachers, giving them the impression that 'What do you want to make a play about?' was a necessary part of the method. As a result I often came across a teacher, with a class with which s/he was very familiar, opening up the Drama lesson with this same question. The result was often chaos because the poor teacher had to work entirely spontaneously. The situation was exacerbated because this group-autonomy trend coincided with the assumption that all drama had to 'hit them in the guts'! All of this meant that, except with the most distinguished teachers, the work was doomed to failure. Today when I teach in schools I still occasionally begin in this open-ended way. That is because it suits me; it should not be seen as part of some approved methodology.

Again an overemphasis on group dynamics distorted what is nevertheless an important characteristic. Not only does drama rely on group interaction in terms of its product, but part of its uniqueness as a learning context stems from the group processes which assist that learning: it provides a unique opportunity for learning from each other.

Successful drama is dependent on positive interaction between group members. Very often a concensus is needed to move the work on, frequently a group can stimulate or dampen the input of an individual, but above all members of the group have to learn to trust each other, *and* they as a group have to learn to trust *drama*. Adolescents who are at a period in their lives when they avoid self-exposure are, not surprisingly, suspicious of an art form that threatens to do just that. Finally, of course, they have to learn to trust the leader of the drama, the teacher. When any one (or more) of these trusts is absent, then *Social Development* becomes a priority (temporarily a 'hard' objective) and once more overrides any aims to do with content/ form.

It is in my experience that the social health of a class can be so negative that Social Development can remain a priority for some considerable time. Obviously one tries to choose both content and form that will enhance that development, but often considerable patience is needed. Because much of the teaching I do is with classes I don't know and/or classes that do not normally do any drama, or who are initially suspicious of my particular approach to drama, I have to content myself with getting the class to trust the novel situation. Sometimes, at the end of one or two lessons, I am not at all sure what they might have learnt in terms of content, but I leave with that positive feeling that comes from recognising that, if we re-meet to work on another project, the necessary degree of trust has now accrued. I have noticed that a recent theoretical writer has little tolerance for this kind of uncertainty from a teacher, in respect of what the class might have actually learnt. I think those of us who are arrogant enough to write books must also have some humility, and appreciate that it is not easy to work in this art form, *as an artist* that is. (To work as an *instructor*, of course, is a very different matter.) Let us never forget that some teachers work under very difficult circumstances, circumstances which may be suffering from destructive group-interaction.

When I teach I am very conscious of the *mood* of a group. Indeed, I find myself responding to the class *as* a group, rather than as a lot of individuals, for the natural dynamics of a group have considerable influence on the group's members: they are often controlled by it. I try to pick up the quality of the 'energy' in a room; I *hear* it rather than see it. (We may differ in this respect: some teachers' perception tends to be visual.) The atmosphere will often guide me in the selection of a focus, and in knowing how to start the lesson sequence. One way in which I differ from many teachers is that, if I am faced with a tricky situation, I assume that I have a better chance to resolve it by getting down to some *drama*, rather than by turning to the ever-popular games or sensitivity exercises. I believe that, by *avoiding* drama, the problem may become exacerbated in the long run, but this is a matter of teacher-style and I have no wish to 'preach' to anyone who has a difficult class.

What I *do* object to is the constant use of games and exercises even when the class is not a problem. Some teachers, especially in North America, seem to bind their students into a routine of preliminary 'warm-up' activities that often turn out to be not so much the *hors d'oevre*, but the whole meal! These exercises are carried out in the name of group behaviour, but I suspect they are there because both teacher and students find them undemanding, and because those teachers would be hard put to know what to do if they couldn't fill up the time with such activities. I wish 'Theatre Games' had never been invented, and as for 'Theatre Sports' ...! Neither of these false trails are likely to give a grounding in good Theatre or good classroom practice. That is not to say I would never use them. For example if I felt my class had been working so hard recently that they needed a break, I might turn to either of these for light relief.

The choice of content is greatly affected by the group as a whole, and the extent to which the *group* is interested in a theme. What you finish up with is often what the more outspoken *leaders* are interested in, until you know your class well, that is, for then you may be able to do something about the problem. One is often dependent on the energy of those same leaders for getting creativity going. Rare are the times when everyone in a group is equally interested in the same theme and equally prepared to bring the same degree of energy to bear on it. Hopefully, as the drama proceeds, there is a chance that the students will all be 'caught' up in it. Just as often, however, the drama proceeds with some of the class as 'passengers' throughout. Again, because we work in an art form, we cannot expect all our students to 'switch on' just because the timetable says they should!

It is not surprising that I have moved into discussing some of the practical problems stemming from group behaviours. As an art, drama depends upon group interaction between actors, and a group statement by actors. I have made the point before that the approach I recommend for classroom drama requires a *collective* starting point. There is a deliberate avoidance, at first, of individual characterisation, but there is often a very firmly implied or stated 'collective characterisation': 'We are all farmers', or 'architects', or 'cavemen'. Always implicit in this is a sense of *collective responsibility borne by the characters*, which goes beyond the individual responsibility felt by the *participants*. This feature of collective characterisation is particularly marked in respect of the Mantle of the Expert approach. Although to the participants the task set (say designing a museum display related to the Bronze Age) appears to be the focus of attention, the teacher uses the task to build up a collective identity of themselves as a firm or agency of designers. It is as if reflected back from the task are implications to do with the agency's past history, reputation, expertise and responsibility. As the group moves to a second and third task, they experience more and more a sense of who they are and what their responsibility is. But more than that, the teacher tries to open up the designers' way of seeing the world: what your eyes tend to pick out if you are a designer; what your priorities tend to be; what you keep and what you discard; what your job *means*. In other words the teacher, in using the M of E approach, attempts to open up for the pupils a whole value system governing expertise.

Theatre knowledge, techniques and crafts

Even as I begin this category, I wonder whether it will be too readily seen as something separate from *Content/form*. Recent theorists and official 'working parties' seem to want to make theatre knowledge and techniques the basis of classroom drama. However, I am cheered by Andy Kempe's *The GCSE Drama Coursebook* (1990). The intention behind this text for older adolescents is clearly to sustain the content/form concept in the minds of the young people as they work. Each page is rich in material, issues and themes to be trans-formed into drama. Text work and non-text work are interdependent, and the three main strands *running parallel* to each other – 'making plays', 'putting on plays' and 'understanding plays' – give further coherence to the notion that substance and form are interrelated. The skills and knowledge about theatre involved are to be acquired *in context*. Each section requires the students to respond to a piece of text and to create work of their own related to a similar theme (not necessarily in that order). [...]

This seems to me to be an ideal way of working in content/form/ technique/ theatre knowledge, with pupils taking an examination in Drama. That it is a *coursebook* naturally has its limitations: there is no teacher available to change the sequence or content to suit the needs of the class and there is no chance for the teacher to take on the occasional role in order to enhance the pupils' work. The wise teacher, of course, will overcome this apparent defi-ciency and use the material of the book in a way that *serves* rather than *binds* the class.

Many of the skills and much of the knowledge identified in Kempe's book (1990) are those related to what I have called 'theatre elements'. These were discussed on p114. But, as one would expect for an examination class, many of the theatre crafts are also included: lighting, design, mask-making, etc. Each of these is to be practised 'in context' as part of content and form, with opportunities for individual students to follow further specialist paths as part of their project work. [...]

Kempe's book is directed at sixteen-year olds, examination classes in parti-cular. It is my purpose in this book to try to ensure that all pupils are given a basic grounding throughout their school life in the art form of theatre. One outcome, but not the most important, will be that sixteen-year olds will take sophisticated text-work and performance in their stride. In addition to the theatre elements already discussed, a number of techniques will be exercised continually from an early age. These may include use of voice, use of move-ment, techniques related to 'illustrating', directing, making a coherent social context, 'reading' a depiction, reading a text for 'subtext', responding spontaneously to each other, responding to *T in R*, etc. Unfortunately there are those who, guided by some recent theorists in the field, will automatically seize such a list and start teaching 'to' it. Such techniques should be *embedded* in content/form (they are all there in my sample sequences of lessons in Chapter 5). However, some teachers will find a way of extracting them from any context and will see them as the equivalent of five-finger exercises, matters for instruction and drill. There will be no one around to tell them what harm they are doing, for even officially appointed 'working party' committees seem to be allowing themselves to be led by the nose in this respect, at least if recent 'working papers' and other official documents are anything to go by. Further, because many of these techniques are related to the performance mode, these same teachers are likely to drop any truly existential experiencing. Again, this is given tacit support by the DES (1989) whose writing gains in confidence when it speaks of dressing-up clothes, electric torches and percussion instruments, as well as '...stage sets, properties, costumes, makeup, stage lighting ...' (*Drama from 5 to 16*, p11) as giving support to techniques of public performance. There is no guidance here as to the maturity of the pupils, just an indiscriminate recommendation to teachers teaching all ages.

However, whereas in *Drama from 5 to 16* the DES (1989) appeared to welcome formal and informal performances by children, their more recent document (1990) does concede that all may not be well:

> In most schools greater emphasis was given to drama at certain times of the year. Christmas, and to a lesser extent Easter, and the festivals and events of faiths other than Christianity were often celebrated in ways which gave a boost to drama. In some schools this was not always a good thing either for drama or for the understanding and enjoyment of the events themselves. This was mainly because they were over-rehearsed, resulting in a stilted, tightly prescribed production.

> Similarly, where classes took turns to conduct assemblies which often incorporated a dramatic presentation, the work was sometimes viewed by the class teacher as an onerous chore requiring much rehearsal and time-consuming effort for little return. In these circumstances the participation rate for many of the children was low, so that too few members of the class really became involved to a serious extent in the performance; the others sat for long periods waiting to take part or simply watched the others rehearse. (Paragraphs 9 and 10)

I have my doubts whether this recent qualification will have much influence on current Arts in schools or Arts Council thinking, for people read what they *want* to read and there is at the moment a vested interest in child performance. This has something to do with the fact that most advisers on official committees are not practising teachers. Perhaps more relevant is the present political climate (I am not talking here of *Party* politics). We are living in a time when the establishment is desperate to go back to 'Education as instruction'. The result is that educational writers in all fields, including drama, are hedging their bets by describing classroom activities in terms that could conceivably be seen as 'instructing in techniques', should that become the new fashion! It is a pity that new faces on the drama scene have not the courage of Peter Slade, Brian Way or Dorothy Heathcote, who were prepared to stand *against* current trends.

It is my belief that development in the basic theatre elements, as described on p114, will ensure that our pupils will be able to approach any aspect of Theatre intelligently and perceptively, not least in respect of responding to the work of dramatists. Unfortunately, the limitations of our culture and educational system often reduce this experience to play-texts rather than to play performances. Rare are the opportunities for our pupils to visit the theatre. Many never see any professional theatre. At least television can sometimes supply good examples of play performance, but under the present economic and Philistine regime, even this possibility is continually being threatened. A serious extension of this exists in the lack of opportunity for *teachers* to see much live theatre. This must inevitably lead to Drama teaching that fails to be sustained by the very source that should be its inspiration.

Note

1 See 'Towards a conceptual framework for classroom acting behaviour' in this volume (p19).

Assessment

This is chapter 7 from *New perspectives on classroom drama*. It is one of the most useful guides to assessment of educational drama that I know of.

I have been among those who have eschewed writing about methods of assessment in drama; anyone having the stamina to comb through my previous books or articles would search in vain for the subject to be given any more than a passing reference. Such neglect does not mean that I have no ideas on the subject. Indeed, that could not be possible, since in my classroom practice I (like every other teacher) apply criteria for assessment continually as a necessary part of the work. I simply haven't felt that I have anything to add to common practice among Drama teachers, just as I haven't felt inclined to give advice to Drama specialists about putting on a school play, important as that is. Likewise I have avoided sounding knowledgeable about 'play corners' in early schooling (I understand a great deal *less* than most reception teachers about this activity). The study of dramatic texts for examination purposes, and even puppetry, might also be added to a quite lengthy list of important classroom activities linked with drama that I have failed to discuss. I make no apologies for this neglect; most writing on education is skewed in the direction of whatever seems in need of elaboration at any one time. However, I have discovered that this 'sin of omission' sometimes seems to give people the impression that neglected aspects are not worthy of attention. In striving to develop an understanding of dramatic playing activity as a structured experience, I have been reacting against two philosophical extremes: the old view that child drama was a matter of 'free' play and the still common assumption that drama activity is to do either with the analysis of texts or with training children as performers ready for the school play.

Some braver souls have already published work on assessment (using the term broadly to include evaluation and attainment targets), but generally speaking their writings suffer from one or more of four critical weaknesses:

1   As I read their advice I cannot 'see' children. That is they are not draw-
    ing on classroom practice as they write, but rather on some philoso-
    phical or aesthetic theories to do with making judgements *about*
    classroom practice.

2   They are too keen (often for political reasons) to find theories that
    embrace *all* the Arts, verbal and non-verbal. They are like a family of
    farmers desperately trying to cover a haystack with a tarpaulin that is
    not quite big enough, so that as they pull it in one direction another
    part of the stack becomes exposed. But as long as they just look at the
    covered area in front of them, they feel confident that the stack is
    waterproofed.

3   Even those few writers who choose to confine their attention to
    drama only are often writing from a narrow frame of reference. They
    turn out to be from a College of Higher Education, from the profes-
    sional theatre or from the Drama department of a Comprehensive
    School. Instead of discussing the assessment of drama with reference
    to what they know most about, their own practice, they purport to
    speak for a wide range of educational experience in drama. Without
    turning a hair, an ex-College of Higher Education practitioner will
    often advise on Primary School practice and its assessment. What is
    offered, of course, is a distorted perspective on what should be done
    with younger children. Working backwards from their knowledge of
    Secondary or Higher Education practice, they assume that younger
    children should be involved in a watered-down version of the same,
    that young children are 'little adolescents' and that their drama ex-
    perience should amount to a preparation for performance theatre.
    Working parties and appointed committees trying to offer the public
    an 'official line' on drama should be wary of their members, whose
    background may be very limited and yet whose current standing may
    be influential.

4   Some Drama specialists writing about assessment still see drama
    practice almost entirely in terms of *acting skills*, and believe that,
    ultimately, 'success' is about playing 'big parts' in school productions.
    Too readily young adolescents are taught quick acting tricks and
    superficial techniques that, if they do pursue an acting career, have to
    be *unlearned* when they get to Theatre School. Yet their assessment
    record may show high grades, given for the veneer of ability the stu-
    dents have acquired. I was talking recently to a Head of Drama in a

Senior High School in Vancouver, British Columbia. She had in one of her Drama classes a student who was picked for a leading role in a film. At fifteen years of age he now felt he had passed the supreme test of ability in drama and did not do any more work on the course. His conception of the course was that it was about being a performer and that he had already reached that particular attainment target!

Some of the principal issues

I shall attempt, towards the end of this chapter, to offer a framework for assessment, but first it is necessary to look in detail at some of the issues. There is one I have continually raised, that of 'learning through drama', but there are others. For instance how does one assess dramatic playing behaviour? Most discussion of assessment seems to assume illustrative/performance behaviour. Even more of a tease is the problem presented to an assessor when the teacher is 'in role'! And what about 'theatre elements' in the dramatic playing work of young children – what is one looking for in terms of assessment? I shall take each of these thorny issues in turn.

Assessment of dramatic playing behaviour

I argued earlier that the dramatic playing activity is initially about creating a social context, just as in any 'life' situation. Following an ethnomethodological perspective, I suggested that in everyday social situations we 'work at' (often unconsciously) making the context we want, so that we can give the social event a suitable label, such as 'a meeting', 'a chat about old times', 'an interview with the boss', etc. Then we often *evaluate* such an event: we speak of a 'good' meeting, a 'successful' interview or a 'pleasurable' chat. This is done on the assumption that the event actually existed and that we have a set of criteria by which we can make judgements objectively.

Although it is recognised that the participants have to *work* to create a social event, it does not follow that it exists only in their minds. There is, in fact, a 'product': a meeting, a chat or an interview. An outside observer could reasonably identify the product according to the actions of the participants. The reason for this is that the only means the participants have of making anything is through the public media of action and language. The *meaning of* what is going on lies in the created product.

This 'making a social context' provides the basis for dramatic playing, and therefore for initial assessment. The product is dependent on the participants having the appropriate resources. These resources are the public media of expression – the actions and language that logically belong to the implicit rules of whatever social event is being created. For example doing drama about 'hospitals' requires the participants to engage in appropriate 'hospital' actions and language. This first step in makebelieve appears to rely on a degree of imitation of the world, especially in its initial stages. One might therefore expect assessment to be straightforward: 'Do they or do they not achieve some resemblance to 'hospital behaviour'?'. Any answer to this question might need to be quite strongly qualified, for a number of reasons:

1   The students' knowledge of hospitals may be inadequate by any reasonable adult standard.

2   Their commitment to this particular drama may be low.

3   An individual in the group may be undermining the work.

4   Although the context is labelled 'hospital', this is but a springboard for another theme, 'hospital' seeming not to be integral to the work.

Either singly or in combination, these kinds of factors raise many questions relating to assessment. I shall discuss each of these points below:

1   If we felt there was an external standard by which we could measure the acceptable degree of resemblance to the 'real' world of hospitals, then anything less would be judged as below that standard. This would be absurd, for knowledge of this kind is relative. Even a 'reasonable adult standard' falls short of a nurse's or consultant's conception of hospital. Likewise a young child's knowledge is likely to be very limited (although I did once in the middle of doing drama on this particular topic discover that we had a son of a surgeon in the class – he took over!). It seems then that in making a judgement about the success with which a group is 'making' a fictitious social context, we have to conjecture what that group might be expected to know. If, for instance, they were five-year-olds we might make a generous allowance. On the other hand, if they were a GCSE examination group involved in creating theatre about hospitals as an examination project, which included performing an excerpt from Peter Nicholls' *National Health* and creating their own 'hospital' drama, then one would expect them to have done adequate research into the subject. Indeed, evidence of their research could be included in their examination folder.

2   We can see that whereas in respect of point 1 the age level of the class is likely to affect the final assessment, lack of commitment to either drama itself or to the particular subject matter may be a characteristic of any age group. Indeed, I have found school headteachers or

principals (or any group where people are anxious to preserve their image) among the most uncommitted groups I have worked with! In practice a distinction has to be drawn between a group which is generally uncommitted, in which case their work will be considered below target, and a group which has lost its commitment to the particular work in hand (perhaps the students have tired of it, failed to become inspired by it, taken on more than they bargained for or, as I shall discuss later, the teacher has structured the work inadequately), in which case, this attitude being untypical of the group, assessment might be waived for that piece of work.

3   It will be noticed that in talking about assessment in Drama, I am making two assumptions: that achievement in terms of content/ form is an immediate issue, and that there is an ensemble responsibility. If we agree that there is a product to be assessed, then we must also agree that it is a collective enterprise. But just as in the 'life' situation a 'meeting' or a 'party' may not be successful because of the detracting behaviour of a minority or individual, so in drama-making one or two can let down the group, either because of recalcitrant behaviour or because of inadequate resources. We all know what it is like to have a young child, in the middle of a drama about Stone Age people, make a reference to watching the television. At such times the teacher makes a swift diagnosis of the cause: is it that the child really doesn't know, or is s/he enjoying upsetting the fiction? S/he also calculates the extent to which the rest of the class is going to be 'thrown' by the inappropriate remark. Indeed, the way the class recovers from the hiatus will be part of the teacher's ultimate assessment of the work. Whether it does or not will often depend on the status of the defaulting member within the natural social hierarchy of the class. If s/he is a natural leader, recovery is less likely. And, of course, any final assessment might well discriminate against that particular child, just as the discrimination will be in favour of the child who helps the rest of the class to a quick recovery. Again, just as in the 'life' situation, one is grateful to the individual who 'saves' the meeting or the party. However, one has to be wary – such situations are rarely black and white. The 'destructive' child in question may be justified in upsetting the fiction, and the teacher may be too blinkered to recognise that it is that particular child's way of protesting, say, that the work lacks integrity. I shall return to the question of assessment of collaborative work at the end of this chapter.

4   The meaning of any social event operates at many different levels. A wedding, for example, will be about many different things according to one's perspective. For the bride and groom, that it is a wedding is central to the experience. This may not be the case for the 'revellers' towards the end of the wedding party. For some people a wedding may be about new friendships struck or enmity reconfirmed. I recently watched a wedding party outside a church in Padua, Italy, where the two sides engaged in a fight that had to be controlled by the police! When young people create a *drama* about a wedding, it sometimes happens that it slides into being about something else, the 'wedding' simply lapsing in importance. This raises questions about the validity of what they are creating, for the art form of drama is dependent on its themes being bound up with the particularity of the context. The theme may centre on revels, new friendships or a fight, but the 'wedding' must somehow remain integral to those themes for it to have dramatic value. In the exploratory approach of dramatic playing it often happens that the drama imperceptibly moves away from its original starting point. When this happens the participants need to have their attention drawn to what is happening, if they do not already realise it. Then they must make a choice between re-establishing the original context or theme and treating the new context as a new beginning. If they begin to stray a second time, this could be considered to be an indiscipline within the group, and the students would be assessed accordingly.

So far I have implied that making a social event in drama is a matter of sending the 'right' signals to each other, for example in the hospital context, doing and saying 'hospital' by: miming appropriate actions; speaking appropriate technical dialogue; demonstrating a respect for hospital hierarchy; creating a mood of dealing with life-and-death matters, etc. Some or all of these may be necessary for the participants to make the context believable to themselves. These are the necessary *descriptive* activities characteristic of the early stages of most social events. The teacher making an assessment does so by bearing in mind the four qualifications listed above.

There is a *second* phase to the dramatic playing mode, a kind of 'gear changing' when the participants move from the 'descriptive' to the 'existential'. When this happens the pupils no longer feel they have to work at making the context believable and real: it *feels* real and *they can submit themselves to it*; they *trust it*; they are free to enjoy its riches; they may find that they draw on resources and talents they did not know they had, and have new insights into what the drama is about. This is the power of the existential moment: it is alive, fluid, open to spontaneous invention and charged with energy. When it is over, however brief it has been, you will have a feeling that you were the author of something real, something authentic, and you will learn by reflecting on it.

Regretfully, many pupils go through their whole schooling without ever having this experience. Many *teachers* who teach Drama have never had a true 'dramatic playing' experience, so do not know what to look for. Many theorists will glibly admit some value to what they often choose to call 'improvisation', without realising that this can be *either* descriptive or existential. Indeed, in North American schools where 'Theatre Sports' have caught on, 'improvisation' in *some* courses has become reduced to 'How slickly entertaining can you be with a mere half minute's preparation time?'. The DES (1990) draws a distinction between 'play', 'role-play' and 'performance'. The difference seems to be one of degrees of formality. There is no acknowledgement of any qualitative differences in acting behaviours. Perhaps it is because they never have the chance to *see* the 'change of gear' I am talking about although, in reading their interesting samples of lessons, one can only assume that part of the success of these exercises lay in the fact that the pupils were, for some of the time at least, operating existentially. I concede, of course, that the two modes can become merged in a way that sometimes leads to inappropriate criteria being applied.

Of course, dramatic playing like any other dramatic form may be of inferior quality. Much that is done in the name of existential experiencing is unworthy and time-wasting. However, we need to understand where the teacher's responsibility lies in respect of the assessment of both descriptive and existential drama. The insightful teacher must be able to recognise when the class is ready to 'shift gear' from the descriptive to the existential. S/he will need to note the extent to which different members of his/her group are able to 'submit' to the fictitious context once it has been made believable. S/he will then observe how effective they are in respect of:

- inventing within the established logic of the context;
- interacting within the group;
- extending their skills, particularly in relation to language and movement;
- responding to *T in R* (if it is occurring);
- handling the art form.

Assessment when the teacher is 'in role'

Whether or not a child can respond to a teacher's role will depend very much on how well the role is set up. I do not mean, of course, how convincingly a character is portrayed but, rather, how securely the ground is laid for the introduction of such a role, and how clearly the idea illustrated by the role is conveyed, for *T in R* behaviour is invariably *descriptive*. An inadequate response by the pupils may be the teacher's fault entirely.

I can recall working with a group of examination pupils in a London Comprehensive School who were studying Ibsen's *An Enemy of the People*. The two sessions of drama I was to conduct were to be filmed by the ILEA camera team. I drew up a careful plan, using the metaphor of a psychiatric hospital. Here the central character in Ibsen's play (Dr Stockmann) was to be subjected to a psychiatric investigation, using psychodrama, by the hospital staff. Members of the class played both hospital staff and other characters in Stockmann's personal and professional life. I was in role as the senior consultant. The *idea* was a good one, but I carried it out in terms of my plan instead of in terms of the class. The students did not know the text as well as I had been led to expect; they were scared of the cameras but anxious to do well in front of them; they were perplexed by this new drama teacher and bewildered by his idea of setting up a psychiatric hospital. Instead of adapting the sequence of their experiences, including my use of *T in R*, to the readiness of the class, and instead of back-tracking when I discovered where they really were in relation to the work, I relentlessly pursued my plan.

Afterwards, I tended to blame the class for not knowing the text, but of course the whole point of the teacher 'in' and 'out of role' is that s/he should adapt the material to suit what is happening. I could easily have set up a series of preliminary experiences that would have allowed the pupils to gain confidence in themselves and in the metaphor, before moving to the major experience within the plan. I failed the class. They still pulled out some good work, but it was not based on an early foundation of trust. So how do we assess our pupils' ability in this kind of circumstance? Do we give the pupils low grades because the teacher set the work up ineptly, or give them high grades because they did well *in spite of* the teacher?!

Having said this, it is still possible to assess a child's general ability in responding to the teacher's contribution. Assuming that what the teacher offers is well-timed, appropriately prepared for and clearly signalled, then differences between the pupils' responses may emerge. The most responsive children in drama will be able to 'read' the teacher's role at a level that goes beyond the 'plot'. Bruner (1971) demonstrated how young children respond to comic strips at differing levels of generality. While some can only respond in terms of 'what happens next', others are able to see social or psychological implications. The same applies to *T in R* which is open to being 'read' at both a surface level and in response to the true 'centre' of what the teacher is offering. The teacher who 'in role' muses, 'Do we have the right to make judgements about people who are worse off than we are?', isn't simply slowing down the decision-making, but is opening up the possibility of philosophical reflection. The dialogue from teacher to young children, 'Suppose we never return? ... That's my front door there ... suppose I never go through it again?', is an attempt to 'deepen' the implications of going on some risky adventure that the class seems to be taking very lightly. Those children who can respond to this new tack introduced by the teacher, and who can further what the teacher has started, are likely to get more out of the drama. It is as though the teacher has moved into a minor key, inviting the pupils to follow. Thus any assessment relates to the child's capacity for seeing the potential, at many different levels, in what the teacher is offering. I call this 'reading', for it has strong links with a child's capacity for reading comic strips, pictures *and* the printed page. Effective *T in R* raises the standard of what is to be 'read'. As I have already emphasised above, the children's ability is dependent on the effectiveness of their fellow artist, the teacher, whose input has to be well-timed and appropriate. The teacher has to sense the 'right' comment and the 'right' question. Morgan and Saxton in their fascinating book (1991) draw the reader's attention to the importance of selecting just the 'right' kind of question and the 'right' style of delivering it.

This process of raising the standard of what is created by appropriate teacher-input is not, of course, confined to dramatic activity. Recently I was watching my granddaughter, Claire, struggling at the age of five to do 'plucking' exercises on her newly acquired violin. She was managing adequately by carefully counting to find the right rhythm and strike the right strings. But when her father provided an exciting 'backing', the piece was 'lifted' into a musical event, and what had been from Claire mechanically correct, now made musical sense. Her whole body expressed the rhythm and she and her father together created music. Her father was doing the equivalent of *T in R* by enhancing the musical experience. This is what Vygotsky (1978) calls the 'zone of proximal development': the development that occurs when the input by an adult helps the learner to achieve beyond their previous capacity.

There are many aspects of the dramatic playing activity that teacher and pupils together will be concerned to assess from day to day. Language, speech and movement are the means by which ideas and dramatic forms are explored. Economy, authenticity and inventiveness are some of the criteria by which one tests standards in these expressive forms.

Assessment of 'illustrative/performance' behaviour

This is, of course, relatively easier to handle than the dramatic playing mode, as the acting behaviour is entirely descriptive. Again, it centres on a combination of form and content. The question the teacher is continually posing is related to the effectiveness of what is being expressed, both in terms of the clarity of ideas and of their expression through the ensemble presentation. A high standard of effectiveness requires that ideas are *uniquely* expressed, that is that the meaning is embedded in the form.

The repertoire of theatre elements already discussed above is just as relevant to the illustrative activity as to dramatic playing. Again, such features as tension and manipulation of space are an *ensemble* responsibility. *Repeatability* is also a characteristic of this 'instant coffee' kind of work. It is not unusual for a teacher or the rest of the class to request, 'Can we see that again?', with a view to re-discussing emerging ideas or re-perceiving subtleties previously missed.

The work is always done for someone else to view. This brings in the responsibility of the *audience* who may act as the 'director' as well as viewers. This introduces what is perhaps a new feature of assessment: it should be assumed that the audience are also working and consequently the way they behave – in offering comments, asking questions, analysing their perceptions, making recommendations, etc. – should be subjected to assessment, whatever the age group concerned. The 'director's eye' and the 'audience member's eye' need to be developed from an early age.

The end-product of illustrative activity is relatively easy to make judgements about, but one wonders to what extent a teacher should take into account the ups and downs of the groups' exploring and rehearsing processes. Sometimes the final piece of work is not what the group is capable of because the participants have submitted to an uncomfortable compromise in the name of consensus. Sometimes the teacher knows that one group is suffering a destructive 'passenger' or an overbearing leader. Alternatively it has been known for a group to have one member whose acting ability is so mesmerising that inadequate work by the others passes unnoticed! These group-dynamic problems are daily teasers for the teacher committed to making honest assessments.

Learning through drama

How do we find out what has been learnt? As I pointed out in Chapter 6 (p.115), in matters to do with understanding rather than with knowledge of skills or facts we are dependent on subtle clues over a period of time. What the pupils have begun to understand they may be unable to articulate, and yet an important shift in the direction of new understanding may have occurred. One can appreciate why some current theorists and practitioners wish to confine appraisal to acting skills, theatre crafts and textual study – they are so much more easily definable and recognisable. But this is to deny why we are doing drama in the first place. Drama must be about engaging with some-thing that matters, and the degree to which our understanding is extended in the art experience is paramount. As assessors we may be guided by the way the pupils are ready to stand apart from their work and *reflect* on what they are creating, either during the process of making it or after it has been made. The reflection may take the form of talking, writing or visual expression; we may also pick up clues from the way pupils apply their new understanding in a different dramatic or 'life' context. Obviously this applies to many different kinds of drama practice, but I suspect that because *T in R* is continually initiating new levels of meaning-making, identification of what the pupils are understanding is particularly hazardous. Sometimes, of course, the teacher can create occasions for reflection *during* the work, breaking off from time to time to test the pupils' grasp on the implications of any 'change of gear'. On the other hand, in the M of E approach there is always evidence of the stan-dard of achievement, for by its very nature this method necessitates *recording* what the participants are doing.

The child's ability to handle the elements of theatre – the child as artist

The significance of the teacher's contribution 'in role' is not, of course, solely a matter of substance: such a contribution should enhance the art of *Theatre*. The teacher may inject elements of Theatre that are absent from the children's own work. Again the question is: 'To what extent can these children 'pick up' and sustain the theatrical element offered through the teacher's role?'.

Important as it is for children to be able to respond to teacher-input, I now turn to a consideration of children's ability to *initiate* dramatic form without the help of the teacher.

About four years ago when my elder granddaughter, Helen, was four-years old, she was scolded by her mother for trying to insist that she ate a Mars bar before her meal. She re-enacted the incident by putting me 'in role' as a 'naughty boy' who must not touch the Mars bar on the shelf behind him. (There was no bar, nor was there a shelf.) As my hand crept in the direction of the supposed shelf, she enjoyed arresting my arm in its progress and delivering a vehement reprimand. After a few times she changed to standing a few metres away and, on each occasion, rushed forward to check her 'naughty boy'. She then discovered (I did not prompt her in any way, I simply, passively, continued the action she wanted me to make) that turning her back on me, pretending to walk away and, finally, appearing to head for the door, all progressively enhanced the excitement of 'catching me in the act'.

This is what I mean by 'understanding' dramatic form. Hers, of course, was not an intellectual understanding; she was probably not conscious of what she was doing, let alone articulate about it. We can only guess at how many similar contexts she would have gone through before she would have stopped 're-inventing the wheel', that is before she could jump straight to the dramatic final step without going through the preliminary exploratory steps. Nevertheless, she demonstrated a knowledge of Theatre shared with dramatists, directors and actors: she selected a clearly defined focus that enabled her to have the experience she wanted; she utilised the difference in status between the two 'characters'; she increased tension by delaying the moment of excitement (arresting my arm); she built tension by manipulating space significantly; and she understood the playwright's art of creating the 'unexpected' by leading my character to be duped by her character's imminent departure – all this in the particularity of the 'forbidden Mars bar/disobedient child context'. The meaning of the experience lies in the content/form combination.

Thus in the pre-school child there is the potential for the very basis of Theatre. The previous anecdote, illustrating as it does the 'existential' mode, demonstrates the manipulation of time and space, the application of constraint, the development of tension, contrast between characters and an element of surprise. I believe most pre-school children have this ability in Theatre. Unfortunately, this natural understanding is often and inevitably allowed to atrophy in the formal school situation. There are a number of reasons for this, listed below:

1   Such activity is left to unstructured play and is not seen by the observing teacher as important.

2   If drama is introduced into the classroom it is often confined to 'illustrative/performance' activity.

3   To expect the child who knows how to harness Theatre in his/her solitary or one-to-one play (as was the case in the anecdote), and to

utilise that same knowledge in small or large-group drama, is to expect the impossible. The new dimension of 'groupness' represents a
huge factor militating against the individual child's natural creativity.
This is not a reason for disbanding drama as a large-group activity,
but it is a reason for teachers to realise that the children will hold their
natural skills in abeyance unless they can be *eased into* the group
dramatic process. *T in R* as a device is almost essential if dramatic
playing is to have dramatic form. Once the children realise that this
form coincides with the theatre resources they already possess, they
will move confidently towards taking the initiative in a large group.

This takes time, however, and groups will vary. Assessment in the Infant
School will relate to where the pupils are in this process of re-learning
dramatic art form. Sadly, some teachers do harness children's natural understanding of Theatre, but in the wrong direction – they encourage the manipulation of time and space and the creation of tension, etc. as part of the young
child's *performance* repertoire. Some influential Comprehensive and Higher
Education teachers believe that training young children to perform in public
is what drama should be about (and some infant teachers are ready to listen
to them). It is so much easier to get young children to jump through performance hoops (I *know*, because this is how I started to teach Drama!) than to
create a rich environment of learning through whole-class dramatic playing.
And, let's face it, teacher-education institutions may not be helping them to
know how to do this.

Finding a framework for assessment

In this and in previous chapters I have emphasised the value of drama as a
medium for conceptual learning. At the same time I drew attention to some
limitations of such a notion. It is difficult to tell:

- exactly *what* has been learnt;
- what *duration* of time is involved;
- what *quality* of learning is occurring.

I pointed out earlier that the participants must not be burdened with the
requirement to learn something. In other words, although in an educational
context a teacher is expected to take full advantage of the learning potential for
his/her pupils, the focus for the participants, it appears, is on 'making drama'
– creating a product. I have slipped in 'it appears' because the phrase, 'making
drama', could be misleading, for it could be construed as offering a way of
looking at drama in the classroom as an *alternative* to learning and under-

standing. There is indeed a danger, in confirming that the participants' goal is 'making drama', that some teachers will interpret this as inviting either free play or theatre skills empty of content.

'Making drama' is just what our pupils *are* doing, but there is also a sense in which drama-making is inescapably linked with learning, understanding and knowledge. We have to find a way of combining the two, a concept that may *imply* an openness to conceptual learning or a change of understanding without that being an explicit *requirement*. It would *also imply* a search for dramatic form. I am suggesting that the phrase 'Drama for meaning-making' might be useful in this context.

Drama for meaning-making

Such a phrase allows the teacher to continue to think in terms of 'What are they learning?'. It steers the participants unequivocally towards content that is important to them, and it also puts drama first.

I believe this provides a more secure base-line, for concepts related to 'learning' and 'change of understanding' can now remain as possible subcategories of 'meaning-making'. While the assessor may or may not have assessable evidence of 'change of understanding' in some of the participants (it will be taken into account if such evidence is there), s/he must expect evidence of attention given by the participants to *the making of meaning*, for meaning-making is what all dramatic activity is about.

We readily make assumptions about 'meaning making' when we read, watch or give a critique of a play. We may explicitly or implicitly ask the question, 'What is the meaning here in this art product?'. Of course, to the question put in this way the answer is always the same: 'The meaning is the art product.'. So, in order to reflect as we read, watch or criticise, we shift the order of the question to something like, 'What *kind* of meanings do we have here in this art product?', or 'Is there a coherent whole?', or 'Does the product make me think?'. These are some of the legitimate questions any theatre-goer or professional critic may ask. They are also legitimate questions in respect of the dramatic 'meaning-making' in the classroom. Thus in classroom assessment you might ask:

- What kind of meanings are there here?
- Is the context created credible to the participants (and to an audience where there is one)?
- Are these kinds of meaning sufficiently significant to the participants?

- Is there evidence of intellectual effort?
- Does what has been created have coherence for the participants (and for an audience where there is one)?
- Does the drama make *me* think?

There is a second type of question the theatre critic poses, related to *theatrical form* – the *how* of the meaning-making:

- What aesthetic forms, metaphor, conventions, styles, genres, characters, focus, context and setting does the playwright employ as vehicles for meaning-making?

These too are legitimate questions to be asked of work in the classroom:

- *How* do these pupils set about making meaning?
- *How* do they negotiate meanings?
- *How* do they sustain and refine them?

In classroom assessment there are two sources of evidence to be taken into account: the 'product' – the drama created – and the 'process' – the experience of the group in achieving the product. Of the 'process' one might ask, for example, 'Did they try out alternative stage-positions for their 'narrator'?' (theatre form) or, 'Did they do any reading round the subject or bring in source material?' (content). Thus the 'what' and the 'how' of meaning-making can be related to both form and content. But, of course, there is a further division to be taken into account: 'Drama for meaning-making' can relate just as much to dramatic playing behaviour as to illustrative/performance behaviour. It is also possible to see dramatic playing both as process and product. Typical 'how' questions for dramatic playing might be: 'Did they take into account ideas offered tentatively, or were they just influenced by the most forceful members of the group?' (process), and 'How did they manage to disguise their suspicions of the disloyal family?' (product). Notice that 'process' questions tend to relate to the participants' experience, whereas 'product' questions relate to the fiction.

I am suggesting that *Drama for meaning-making* can provide us with a coherent framework from which to operate assessment. In the *broadest terms* the following questions would be posed:

Questions related to content:

- What kinds of meanings are here?
- Is there evidence of conceptual learning?

Questions related to form:

- How have these kinds of meaning been achieved?
- Is there evidence of cognitive and social skills (thinking, questioning, listening to each other, etc.) being acquired?

In each case these questions should be applied to:

- process and product;
- dramatic playing and illustrating/performing.

The process of assessment is hugely complex. I hope that the above suggested framework will provide a base-line that will cater for a wide range of dramatic activities. Many of the issues discussed earlier in this chapter should now fall into place within this frame.

'Grading' a group

I tend to follow a particular procedure for grading group work which the reader may be interested in. I am sure other teachers have methods that are just as useful, but I thought there was no harm in sharing what I do.

There are many times when, as the examiner or as the teacher, I am presented with the end-product of a group's work, work which has perhaps taken several weeks to prepare. As examiner, of course, it is probable that I do not know the participants. I begin by making a private categorisation of the *product*. I assess what I see of the outcome by giving the work, say, a C if that is assumed by the institution to be average, an A if I thought it was distinguished, and a D if I thought it was less than satisfactory, etc.

I invite the students (before they see my grades) to grade each other, using the criteria of a person's technical ability, their resourcefulness in terms of ideas, and their commitment to the work. The two latter, of course, apply to the whole process over a period of time. If it is a large class, instead of having each person graded I may ask them in a secret ballot to nominate any members they feel have distinguished themselves, or failed to pull their weight. They are also asked to grade themselves. I then adjust my general category grading, applying minuses and plusses in a way that can stretch individual results outside that category. Thus it is conceivable for a C-graded product to have within it individuals with an A- and an F+. Students I have done this with seem to regard it as a fair way of working. It always astonishes me how much agreement there usually is within a group, especially in respect of which students should be given an A.

Continuous assessment

The Caloustie Gulbenkian Foundation (1982) recommends daily assessment, a feature of Canadian and American schools. My experience in those countries makes me feel reluctant to approve it as a practice, for in so many of their classrooms each child feels subjected to continual observation and grading by the teacher. The outcome is inevitably that the students come to see Drama as *about assessment*. The focus of attention is not directed towards 'meaning-making' as artists, but on whether or not the student will get an A for a particular piece of acting. So intent are students to catch the teacher's eye that their acting behaviour is automatically orientated towards the illustrative/performance mode, even when they are supposed to be behaving 'experientially', and if the teacher is looking the other way there seems to be little point in 'busting a gut'!

Yet the intention behind regular, illuminative, informal assessment seems sound. It is, after all, what we are doing most of the time we teach. Perhaps the mistake in North America is that such daily evaluation tends to be linked to grades. I think this is avoidable provided pupils understand from the beginning of a course that the idea of 'grading everything' is firmly excluded. We also need to find a form of continual assessment that gives credit to the participants' self-judgement. Only then can they begin to see themselves as artists in the classroom.

Constraint

An extract from Chapter 4: 'Teacher as Fellow Artist – Working from 'Outside the Drama" in *New Perspectives on Classroom Drama*. The notion of constraints in drama is one of the most useful notions for the drama teacher to have at her/his disposal.

When I first studied drama seriously, one of the 'laws' that was drilled into me was that 'drama is conflict'. In subsequently running workshops in drama I faithfully followed this ideal by setting mother against son, brother against sister, town against town, state against state, and tribe against tribe. My workshops were characterised by the volume of vociferous hostility permeating the theatre studio, school hall or classroom. It was only on an occasion when we slipped into an improvisation where two parents were anxiously waiting for bad news, that it dawned on me that we had something intensely dramatic on our hands that had little to do with conflict.

Since then, through a study of play-texts, I have realised that what playwrights are really concerned with are constraints. Obviously, conflict is a necessary part of drama, but the expression of conflict is no more important, and indeed may be less important, than the withholding of it. If two people want to express their hostility or love towards each other, but for some reason are not free to do so, that can be more dramatic than their giving full vent to their feelings: in Shakespeare's *Twelfth Night*, Viola cannot declare her love for Orsino – when she does the play is over; in Shakespeare's *King Lear*, Goneril and Regan cannot explicitly declare to their father, 'We want to be rid of you' – they disguise their true feelings by appearing to be concerned about the size of his entourage. In most texts one or more characters are constrained in the expression of true feeling. On those rare occasions when there is virtually no constraint, either the whole play or that part of the play is over, or you can be sure that the audience knows or guesses that such an honest interaction cannot last, or that is is falling short in some way of being a true expression. Even the continual raging of the husband and wife in Albee's *Who's afraid of*

Virginia Wolf? turns out to be a shared expression of pain at the couple's childlessness.

More common even than constraint on self-expression is the constraint on true facts being exposed. This provides the dynamic, from a typical 'Who-dunnit?' to *Oedipus Rex* where the whole play is given to a gradual unfolding of the truth. Another common form of constraint is the setting up of obstacles so that a character cannot do what s/he wants to do. In vain, Macbeth seeks supreme power. These two constraints, the withholding of facts and the inhibition on a character's wants, provide the substance for a play's plot. It is, however, the first kind of constraint mentioned above, the constraint on expression of feeling, that is of particular interest to workshop leaders and participants, for this kind of constraint affects the dynamic of every momentary interaction and so is relevant to even the briefest improvisation exercise.

We can attempt a categorisation of the constraints on true expression of feeling. They appear to be:

- physical;
- psychological;
- social;
- cultural;
- procedural;
- formal or technical.

These are not discrete divisions: it is not always possible to distinguish between what is psychologically and socially determined, or between what is socially and culturally determined. Nevertheless, it is useful for a teacher to separate them for they can provide the basis for selecting a workshop exercise. I shall now look at the typical 'pairs' exercise described at the beginning of this chapter, to be carried out by a class of adolescents, using the well-tried theme of 'angry parent greets offspring who had promised to be home an hour ago'. It will be obvious that the choice of constraint brings a distinctly different texture to the experience.

Physical constraint
The parent has to vent his/her anger through the shut and locked door of the bedroom to which the offspring has rushed on arrival.

Psychological constraint

The parent is determined, for the sake of their future relationship, to control his/her angry feelings.

Social constraint

The parent is embarrassed because of the presence of a visiting relative, who has nobly offered to 'wait up' with the parent.

Cultural constraint

Because it is past midnight it is now the day of the parent's birthday, and the adolescent has brought home a birthday present!

Procedural constraint

The late daughter happens to be the Queen of England!

Formal or technical constraint

The offspring is totally deaf and relies on sign language, or the scene is to take place using animal characters as a metaphor – between 'parent rabbit' and 'adolescent bunny'!

Constraints have a pedagogical as well as dramatic implications. The drama lies in the constraint (often, you will notice, having a moral implication) on the character, but the participant, or actor, can also 'enjoy' the meaningful tension between the spoken and the unspoken. Paradoxically, it is the un-spoken that is brought to mind because expression of it is not allowed. The teacher in the classroom can harness this paradox, for it means that the adolescent or adult participants can engage with themes like 'facing death', 'grief' or 'love' at a sub-focal or tacit level, while their focus of attention is on not expressing grief or love, etc. This means that 'heavy' material for impro-visation that would normally be avoided, because the participants would tend to trivialise it rather than explicitly deal with it, can be tackled with the knowledge that it is to remain implicit. In this way, far from the theme be-coming trivialised, it can be engaged with in safety at whatever level each participant is ready to cope with.

Imagine, for example, that the students are going to play the characters of the parents, grieving over the loss of their daughter. By insisting on some relevant constraint, such as 'refusing to talk to each other', 'silently blaming each other' or 'having to stay bright for the sake of the other daughter', there is a greater chance that not only will the scene be dramatic, but it will also be significant to the participants. They may get much nearer to a sense of grieving because they are not required to express it.

Breaking the constraint: temporary chaos!

If constraints are in themselves dramatic, then it is certainly true that 'breaking' them is equally dramatic. In Shakespeare's *The Winter's Tale*, Leontes eventually cracks and banishes Hermione from the court; late in Miller's *Death of a Salesman*, Willie Loman painfully hears the truth from his son; in Shakespeare's *King Lear*, Lear is banished into the storm; Shakespeare's *Hamlet* turns on Ophelia; Shaw's *Pygmalion* is about that most common social constraint: social status, and Eliza Doolittle eventually has the guts to break it. To persist with a constraint too long is to lose the dynamic of the drama. For this reason, in the classroom, the teacher setting up a pairs exercise may place a strict limit on the time allowed, knowing that if a constraint is over-sustained the drama will disappear. At other times, however, the pairs may be 'empowered' to move the scene towards a more explicit mode of expression from one or more of the characters: the 'parent' of the late child 'loses' his/her temper in spite of the constraint; the grieving parents find a way of talking about the death of their daughter. For a dramatic playing exercise to include this 'change of gear' towards explicitness, and for it to be effective, the participants must be sensitive to both when and how to carry out this change. Obviously the transformation can only be a dramatic one if the experience of the constraint has been sufficient, both in terms of tension and duration.

The teacher of drama must help students to achieve the relevant skills of selecting, constructing and breaking constraints. These will in turn help the students to work on scripts, for the application of the notions of 'constraint' and 'breaking the constraint' will not only affect the way teachers and students prepare and reflect upon their dramatic playing exercises, it will also provide them with a new and interesting way of looking at written texts. One can 'hear' the restraint on both characters at the beginning of the following scene between Hamlet and his Mother:

> HAMLET: Now, mother, what's the matter?
>
> QUEEN: Hamlet, though hast thy father much offended.
>
> HAMLET: Mother, you have my father much offended.
>
> QUEEN: Come, come, you answer with an idle tongue.
>
> HAMLET: Go, go, you question with a wicked tongue.

Both are testing the ground, both afraid of what will be said, of what will be done. But towards the end of the scene, as the rawness of the Queen's guilt and of Hamlet's contempt become exposed, they both lose hold of their constraint:

> QUEEN: O Hamlet, speak no more.
> Thou turn'st mine eyes into my very soul,
> And there I see such black and grained spots
> As will not leave their tinct.
>
> HAMLET: Nay, but to live
> In the rank sweat of an enseamed bed,
> Stew'd in corruption, honeying and making love
> Over the nasty sty!
>
> QUEEN: O speak to me no more.
> These words like daggers enter in my ears.
> No more, sweet Hamlet.
>
> Shakespeare, *Hamlet* Act III Scene IV

I have suggested that this kind of exercise, requiring pairs of pupils consciously to employ a constraint imposed by the teacher, is not suitable for young children. Many of them will already have an unconscious understanding of theatre form, observable in their 'free' play, but having to carry out a teacher-imposed 'constraint' task is likely to be too much of a straight jacket for them.

This kind of knowledge about how theatre works can also be applied to pupils' illustrative/performance activities, where an interaction (that is, not a still picture) occurs between two or three participants. The teacher, working from the 'outside', can be actively engaged in going round the groups as they prepare their performances, or when the whole class is directing 'guinea pigs' at the front. S/he can prompt the participants to apply constraints on what the characters say to each other in order to make their work more theatrically exciting. When a performance is over the teacher can usefully lead a discussion about the validity of the kind of constraint (psychological, social, etc.) chosen by the characters, and the extent to which the 'audience' were made aware of the 'hidden truth' of the situation, in spite of the constraint. Of course, if the performance includes a character no longer able to sustain the constraint, such matters as the timing of the fracture, how it occurred and the outcome are all relevant matters for reflection. As I have said, this kind of knowledge will also allow pupils to probe scenes from play-texts.

Protection

From *Drama as education*, Chapter 6 'Emotion and the game of drama', dealing with the very important process of protecting children into role when the material is potentially challenging.

I cannot stress enough how important it is for teachers to realise that be- cause drama is such a powerful tool for helping people change, as teachers we need to be very sensitive to the emotional demands we make on our students. The notion of 'protection' is not necessarily concerned with protect- ing participants *from* emotion, for unless there is some kind of emotional engagement nothing can be learned, but rather to protect them *into* emotion. This requires a careful grading of structures toward an effective equilibrium so that self-esteem, personal dignity, personal defences and group security are never over-challenged. I shall discuss three kinds of protection: (a) perfor- mance mode, (b) indirect handling of the topic and (c) projection.

1 Performance mode

Performance mode has its own kind of built-in protection. One way of using it, as we have already discovered, is to treat the pain of a funeral gathering as a technical exercise. In other words, instead of trying to simulate grief or whatever, the emotional aspects are held in abeyance in order to make decisions about the external features of the depiction. There are many advan- tages of working this way, two of which are that the performance technique required is minimal, well within the abilities of the class to achieve a satisfactory result from their point of view, and that it allows the class and its individual members to control the emotional input. If they wish they can stick to the bare bones of the task, as an intellectual exercise, but if they feel secure they may inject 'feeling' ideas.

The second structure, involved in the line of dialogue round the graveside, is more exposing, for it really tests each participant's commitment to the affec- tive aspect of the event. But each is still strongly protected by the very form of the performance mode. It is stylised, abstract. It would have been far more threatening to have attempted a simulation of a 'round the graveside' dramatic playing.

Briefly, then, for we shall be returning to this same point later in the book, it can be said that the performance mode itself can be protective, either because it is seen to be mainly a technical or intellectual task, or because the dramatic form is powerful enough to enhance whatever the participants' contribution might be. Sometimes the strong sense of form causes individuals to rise to the occasion or if they do not, their inadequacy can be contained by the form itself.

2 Indirect handling of topic

Some subjects are painful, sensational, controversial or just a bit too exciting. This is not a reason to avoid them for drama more than any other activity in school can help children find a mature approach to such topics. But to handle them *directly*, that is, to open up the central issue that arouses the pain, sensationalism or the controversy is not necessarily the best way of protect-ing children into emotion. Indeed, with some topics if the teacher does not handle them indirectly, the class will hastily protect themselves by opting out, fooling around, etc.

There are three ways of dealing with a topic indirectly. One is to enter a drama at an oblique angle to the main issue. For instance, I recall David Davis being asked by his class of adolescents if they could do some drama about prostitu-tion. After discussing what led a girl to become a prostitute they then set up a series of dramas showing some of the stresses (including poverty) a fictitious character had had to face in her early life.

Likewise, in setting up a drama for an already excitable ten-year-old class on their chosen topic of a haunted house, I spent the whole of the first lesson as a pub proprietor refusing to show them how to find the house. Of course, such a device is doing more than protecting them from an over-exciting adventure; it is also in a calmer way building up their anticipation of a real mystery. For these young children the haunted house gained in significance as they tackled the immediate problem of the bloody-minded landlord – just as in the 'prostitution' lessons a more respectful attitude to the problems of prostitution grew as the adolescents actually centred their attention on 'where poverty can hurt'.

Another, more popular, way of working indirectly is to place the participants in a role that only obliquely connects with the topic. Dorothy Heathcote is very fond of employing this structure. 'Mantle of the expert' for example, is almost by definition a way of working from an angle of detachment. (Protection is not its only value, of course – others will be discussed in the final chapter). Thus in our 'suicide' drama the adolescents, instead of being in role as members of the family concerned, could have been neighbours or reporters getting a good story. In the 'prostitution' lesson, instead of being in role as the 'other poor people' sharing the girl's life, they could have been social workers, town councillors or students on a counselling training course. The 'haunted house' drama could have had its 'investigators from the British Poltergeist Society'.

A third way of dealing with a topic indirectly, perhaps the most difficult to handle, is to use *analogy*. It is difficult, for any misjudgement in the planning by the teacher can seriously affect the validity of the parallel that is being drawn. The simplest form of analogy is to change the historical setting for the event, for instance, attempting to place The Good Samaritan in a contemporary setting, or doing the reverse of this – taking some contemporary problem such as racism and setting it in past times, in a context between, say, the Jews and the Samaritans or the Greeks and the Romans. On the other hand, the apparent dissimilarity can be stretched even further (say, using the Odysseus and the Sirens story for the topic of drug abuse) providing the teacher takes care to ensure the group makes the right connections!

3 Projection in the dramatic playing mode

Central to Peter Slade's theory of child drama was the distinction he made between personal and projected play (or drama). He writes:

> Throughout the whole of life, Man is happy or unhappy in so far as he discovers the right admixture for his life of these quite distinct manners of using energy. Both the type of person and the life occupation are connected with the balance of Self and projection. (Slade, 1954:35)

It is his recognition that projected activities draw upon a distinctly different kind of energy (and I include emotional response) from non-projected activity that I think is of fundamental importance. His classification into personal and projected play represents a hierarchy of abstraction; dramatic activities using oneself as the medium of expression standing at a lower level on the table of abstraction than dramatic activities using media other than oneself. I would like to extend his thesis in order to establish that the dramatic playing mode can use both personal and projected activity. To avoid confusion of terms, I prefer to refer to the activities as either projected or 'non-projected'. A hierarchy table could look like this:

	A	The activity of running	Concrete (no abstraction)
NON-PROJECTED	B	Running to hide as part of a game	first level of abstraction
	C	Running 'as if' in a drama	second level of abstraction
	D	Running in a mime performance	second level of abstraction
PROJECTED (ACTIVE)	E	Drawing a runner Sculpting a runner Making a sound tape of running feet Writing a story about a runner Directing a mime performance of running, etc.	higher levels of abstraction
PROJECTED (PASSIVE)	F	Looking at a photograph of a runner Handling a sculpture of a runner Reading about a runner Watching a play or a film about a runner, etc. etc.	higher levels of abstraction

Let us take the activity of running.

It is the projected activities, the group under E and F, which will concern us in this section, as we shall see that it is projection which protects the participants. I have divided E and F according to whether they are actively engaged in projecting, i.e. either making something or merely percipients of a 'running' stimulus, a much more passive role. Quite obviously the passivity of, say, looking at someone else's drawing is considerably less demanding than doing one's own. Both are projected activities, for in each case one's attention is directed away from oneself, which is of course what offers the protection.

(a) Passive projection

Examples might include having case-study documents of the new intake available as a starting point for a drama about prison; a huge map for a drama about Treasure Island; and architects' designs of Paris sewers for a drama about a bank robbery. ... The list can go on and on: contents of a hand-bag; pages of a diary; newspaper cuttings; an epitaph; school record cards; photographs of housing demolition; map of a street; artifacts of any evocative kind.

An important extension of this 'passive' list is Dorothy Heathcote's use of a second 'person-in-role' (in addition to the teacher) – a tramp, a soldier, a stowaway, Christopher Columbus, etc. One of the advantages of using a person-in-role over inanimate objects is that the 'passive' stage of watching and listening can gradually change to a more active involvement, as and when the class seems ready, but more important of course is the extra dynamic edge that is brought to the whole occasion by having present someone real and breathing and tangible instead of just a photograph. One can use both of course. Chris Lawrence, in working with a class of London children, showed them some photographs of 'dancers' whom the children were later to meet and instruct on the movement of animals. The class spent considerable time examining these photographs, attempting to anticipate the kind of personalities they were to be working with. Such is found to be the effectiveness of having a second person-in-role (usually another teacher) that Newcastle upon Tyne Drama Advisory Team have cultivated the idea of offering a 'character' to the local schools (they call it 'Rent-a-role', so that a class in a primary school, say, working on the topic of The Peasants' Revolt can – with sufficient notice of course! – ask one of the team to come into the school as Wat Tyler). One of the most fully documented projects of this kind is Dorothy Heathcote's (1980) work with a nine-year-old class on Dr. Lister (see also *The Treatment of Dr. Lister by John Carroll* (1980)).

It will be seen that the variations on this passive kind of projection are infinite. It does not, of course, have to be the first stage of the drama work. Injecting a different perspective of this kind part way through a project can also have its uses. The important point is that it should be used at a time when for some reason pressure is to be taken off members of the class – putting them in what is virtually a 'spectator' role can give them time to recover from what had perhaps been inadequate non-projected work. I say *virtually* a spectator role, for the teacher is likely still to endow the pupils with a role label – 'I have a patient outside. I have asked you senior staff here for a special reason. I would like you to watch me interview him' – immediately lets the class off the hook of having to participate in the normal way. Notice they are not only given a *reason* for observing, which, of course, gives their spectator role a frame through which to watch, but there is also a hint of some responsibility they might have to carry – a necessary engagement is then ensured.

(b) Active projection in dramatic playing

It would be less passive, but still a form of projection, if in the above illustration I were to add, 'And doctors ... if you wouldn't mind making notes ... to help our discussion later'. In doing this I have further controlled the quality of attention to be expected *but* it still protects the participants because the centre of their attention is away from themselves. Likewise, if instead of saying, 'there is a patient outside', I could say (out of role), 'In a short while I will be a patient coming to the consultant's office – how do you want me to play the role? For instance, when I am sitting on this chair, how do you want me to appear? etc., etc.' (I recently watched a more formal version of this technique where a class of adolescents was invited to direct the teacher in how to appear as a King of a small Greek State in classical times who had lost his power to a conquering neighbouring state but who did not want to lose his dignity. The group would be more than spectators for now they have to make active decisions. Their attention is still projected – in this case through the 'modelling' they are doing on the teacher.) There is, of course, an enormous difference between the private/public demands of the two examples: writing my own private notes protects me rather more than having publicly to make suggestions on how the teacher as 'patient' should, say, knock on a door. The teacher who knows her class will judge best which of these projections the class will be most comfortable with or will be most challenged by. For the other side of the 'protection' coin to be wary of is over-protection.

In the illustrations of projection so far I have suggested that broadly speaking there are two kinds: (1) where the participants are allowed to be passive observers becoming more actively engaged as and when they wish, and (2) where from the beginning the participants are required to *do* something. Both of these strategies can keep non-projected dramatic playing at bay for a long time if necessary. I can recall a class of ten-year-olds designing their own Norman village for several drama sessions before they became engaged in non-projected drama activity (personal play, as Peter Slade calls it), i.e. before they started interacting with each other as *villagers* instead of *through their designs*. Notice both activities qualify as dramatic playing for both carry the intention to 'be', to be either designers or villagers, both working spontaneously and appropriately within their quite different functions.

It is not always easy to switch from projected to non-projected drama. The projected can feel so secure – there is often so much less personal risk in being in role as a 'head teacher' examining and discussing case-study documents of a school truant than being involved in 'reprimanding a school truant'. One of the ways of making a bridge between the two is to use teacher-in-role.

(c) Teacher-in-role

The most subtle strategy available to a teacher is that of teacher-in-role, for this device is flexible enough to have any one of the three functions; it can take the pupils' attention *off* themselves by allowing them passively or actively to use teacher's role as a projection, or it can be non-projective and challenge the pupils to interact. It is relatively easy to move from one to the other. I can give an illustration of what I mean. When I asked a class of five-year-olds what they would like to 'turn me into' for a story, they said a witch, and added, a very wicked witch. Thus they had a chance *actively* to project onto me whatever 'wickedness' they had in their minds. I did not carry out their instructions very well so they had to be very precise in explaining things to me. Some of their instructions included reading a spell-book in my witch's house, which had, we established, a door close to where the children were sitting.

I moved to a different phase and involved myself in witch-like pursuits, looking for a special spell (they had already told me what it was to be). Thus, for a few moments they reverted to *passive* projection, in role merely as spectators of teacher's performance. Now my responsibility is to bring them a non-projected activity. The remarkable thing about teacher-in-role is that it allows the teacher to change into a different gear, as it were, as subtly or as crudely as the occasion seems to require. In this particular instance, I casually 'looked through my window' and muttered to myself that I thought I saw 'some people' outside my house. This single action and comment implied a huge transformation in but one simple step, for suddenly we were on the edge of non-projected activity – 'some people outside my house' places the children in a markedly different relationship to the drama. They are in danger of losing their spectator status. The tension rises as they sense the difference. I moved to the door and 'opened it' an inch. They felt very threatened, although 'opening the door of my house' had been one of the actions tried out when the class was directing me in how to be a witch. But the meaning has changed, for now *they* are included in 'dramatic time' and are much less protected. Notice how the first step of looking through the window is less threatening than the second one of opening the door. The window distances to some extent; the door exposes the alarming feeling of not only sharing the same dramatic time but the same dramatic space. So I 'open it *an inch*' and thus I delay further, giving them time to take it all in and to adjust to the exposure to what they must ultimately cope with: the witch addressing them directly. This careful bridging from projection to non-projection is yet another skill a teacher needs to acquire.

Thus the teacher-in-role can decide from moment to moment whether to carry the burden of the pupils' protection – 'My men (a group of 'passive' children) have *this* to say to you' is to be totally protective – or to remove that protection and hand over the power: 'My men have something to say to you ...!' Let us conclude this section on protection by tabulating our analysis.

Protective techniques

Performance:	Technical
	Formal
Indirect:	Oblique approach to topic
	Distanced role
	Analogy
Projection:	Passive
	Active
	Teacher-in-role

Let us look at a sequence in a recent series of lessons with the Vancouver children already referred to earlier in this chapter. In the first session the group chose the topic of hospitals in the future. Three phases in the first lesson were as follows:

(1) Designing, in small groups, some special machines to be found in hospitals in the future.

Because they were not enacting any kind of simulation of hospital life, the exercise could be described as INDIRECT.

It was also indirect in respect of role distance – they were 'designers', not part of hospital life. Because their concentration was actively on something other than themselves it could be described as ACTIVELY PROJECTED.

(2) The class was asked to instruct me and one of the pupils in how to behave as a reporter and doctor respectively, the reporter wanting information from the busy doctor about 'these new machines' he had heard about.

This has moved into the DIRECT – a doctor who is using one of the machines is involved. But it remains as ACTIVELY PROJECTED – a totally different kind of projection, of course.

(3) Half the class became 'doctors' and half remained as 'designers'. A public discussion was held between the groups, the designers explaining how the machines would work.

This is an extension of the scene they had directed at 2, but they were now all in it.

The finished designs, although offering partial projection were not sufficient to take away the focus of attention from the participants themselves, for they were now all in 'dramatic time'. This was therefore DIRECT AND NON-PROJECTED.

These are three simple and fairly obvious examples of protective devices with a topic that did not of itself require careful handling, but when at the end of the lesson they chose to extend their interest in hospitals in the future to 'finding a cure for cancer' quite suddenly the subject-matter has become more of a delicate one, with some taboos attached for both the pupils and the adults watching the lesson. Thus in my planning for subsequent lessons, the person in the drama who might die of cancer *was never played by anyone in the group*. A chair was placed in a certain spot in the room for each lesson – Theresa's chair. Theresa was a six-year-old girl who was going to need our scientific skill and our love. We saw her doll, always with her on the arm of the chair, but Theresa was never there. She *became there* as the week went on and as we seriously, intently were able to talk to her and even comb her hair.

We built up a *projection* of Theresa, and Theresa's cancer became very real. This is what I mean by *protection* – we did not run away from the terrible topic: the use of projection allowed us to *face* cancer.

Summary

In this chapter we have argued that emotion in drama is real, but that it is nevertheless a modified version of that same emotion felt in an actual event, for the emotional response in drama is a response to an abstraction. It is also accompanied by the dual affect of satisfaction in creating the drama. The emotion felt, although heavily qualified, can be equally or even more intense, as for all second-order experiencing.

For a child to feel free to respond to a make-believe situation, there must be sufficient signals in the environment reminding him that the real world continues to exist. 'Submitting' to the experience is a necessary step which a participant may be deterred from taking for a number of reasons, particularly if he has too great a vested interest in the subject-matter or in his own reputation.

According to Tormey's theory of expression, emotional involvement for the actor is minimal. Such a theory would seem to support the notion of two distinct orientations of dramatic playing and performing, but Stanislaysky's theory of acting seems to embrace both modes, leading us to consider the model as *dialectic*, each mode containing the seed of its opposite. In looking, therefore, for a possible performance element within the dramatic playing mode we discovered that a certain heightened form of dramatic playing, which we labelled *presentation*, occurred when a significant contribution by a participant was communicated by words and gestures achieving a shared public meaning. At such moments participants find their 'public' voice and do not need the kind of protection they may have relied on earlier.

We discussed the concept of 'protection' as protection *into* emotion not from emotion. We looked in some detail at some aspects of protection which included certain kinds of technical and formal *performance*, the *indirect* handling of painful subjects and *projection*, the latter including some aspects of the teacher's most flexible strategy, *teacher-in-role*.

Drama and meaning

This article, from *Gavin Bolton: selected writings*, was written for a British Council course organised by Dorothy Heathcote in September 1982 for a group of 20 visitors from all over the world.

It has become quite fashionable among teachers in the UK in recent years to talk about drama education in terms of *Meaning*. Ever since the Schools Council Drama Project authors (McGregor *et al*, 1977) gave us their sociological perspective on drama teaching and built their theoretical framework around the notion of 'negotiation of meaning', the significant content of a drama lesson which in the past might have been thought of as dramatic skills or life-skills or social skills or free-expression is now centred on the drama's meaning. 'They must focus on the meaning of the drama and then the subsidiary actions will come right and true,' says Dorothy Heathcote in *Exploring theatre and education* (p29) edited by Ken Robinson (Heinemann, 1980). One of the problems is that we lack a sophisticated language for describing the meaning of an experience either as a participant or as a teacher/observer. And it may be, as this paper will attempt to show, that whether or not the meanings are the same for both the participant and the teacher/observer depends on the kind of drama practised. A further attempt will be made to demonstrate that fundamental differences in philosophical positions can determine the *levels* of meaning available to both parties.

We have not entirely lacked a terminology for discussing meaning in drama, for traditionally we have employed a literary categorisation distinguishing levels of meaning. The distinction is often drawn, for example, between *Plot* and *Theme*. By the former we mean a sequence of particular events; by the latter a more generalised level of meaning is intended, a higher order of abstraction of human behaviour of which the particular events are an instance. I would like to add a third level, that of *Context*, which refers to the chosen physical situation: place, period or idiom in which plot and themes evolve. Thus reducing Hamlet to its crudest terms, the *Plot* is a sequence of deaths; a *Theme* is Revenge; and the *Context* is the Royal Court of 17th-century Elsinore.

The levels of meaning of a novel could be set down in similar ways. The difference for drama, however, is that events take place in space and time through simulated action. Does this suggest then that the meanings can actually be *seen* in action? To what extent is it possible to claim that the various meanings can be observed? The question is relevant for the theatre critic and drama teacher alike, but as we are concerned here with drama teaching, let us confine our thinking to drama created by teacher and children. It is not difficult to transfer the literary categorisation to children's work. For instance, in a drama about unemployment, the Plot is, say, about a man being made redundant applying for another job; the Context is an 'interview situation'; and one of the Themes (*or* 'learning areas' using educational jargon) could be 'Self-esteem'. Are Plot, Context and Theme directly observable? The most obviously accessible of these seems to be the Context. Certain features of an interview situation would have to be overtly represented if the drama is to have any validity at all. And in so far as each action is seen to have coherence with its preceding and subsequent actions, the story-line of 'what is happening now and what will happen next' is certainly made explicit. So far, then, we can confirm that at least the levels of meaning, the Plot and the Context, are largely observable from the action. And although the angle is different, presumably in many instances of drama activity teacher/observer and participants could reasonably agree about those particular levels of meaning.

At this point we can note that there are at least two kinds of drama teaching where the priorities of the teacher are such that one or other of these two meanings entirely fulfils the teacher's educational requirement. The drama often referred to as *Simulation* (I am not using the word here as Dorothy Heathcote tends to use it) requires that the participants learn something about a particular situation in the world – for instance, how a large factory is organised; how to use a telephone; how decisions are made in Local Government; how law courts operate etc. When drama is used in this way to teach precisely about how something is done or should be done, it is eminently proper that the total concentration of the participants and the teacher should be on effective representation of the Context: when you are teaching young children about Road Safety you do not want them to finish up learning about something else! Less admirable, however, are the educational objectives of the teacher whose sole interest is in accurate representation of a Plot. This regrettable emphasis is still found among teachers of young children in particular. Story-line is given undue significance and treated as if it is the only meaning available. The children finish up 'knowing' the story but oblivious to any other level of meaning. Jerome S. Bruner, in *The relevance of education* (Penguin Educational, 1974) writes of children deprived of access to a 'deeper meaning'. He is not speaking of drama but the same point is being made. He is talking about how different children 'read' comic strips: *Pogo* and *Little Orphan Annie*. 'Either can be read in terms of 'what-happened-that-day'. And probably a fair number of children read the strips in just that way. But one can read each with a sense of its form, its social criticism, its way of depicting human response to difficulty, its underlying assumptions about the dynamics of human character.' (p104) Unwittingly, some teachers use drama to train children to stay with the obvious – that which can be made explicit through action.

And yet, left to themselves, those same children might well choose not to make explicit in their drama either the plot or the context. Shipwrecks without a sea or even without a ship are not uncommon, and to an observer the plot can remain curiously obscure! Thus it would have been more correct in the earlier paragraph to have qualified the assertion that at least two levels of meaning are 'largely observable', for sometimes plot and context can remain in the participants' minds and may not *necessarily* be depicted by the action. A word of caution is needed here however. By saying that something is occurring '*in the mind' rather than in the action* I am in danger of perpetuating a philosophical heresy I have no wish to support. I could be quite rightly charged with *dualism*, that is separating mind and body, implying that the mind does one thing and the body something different. We need to look a little closely at this particular problem, for strange as it may seem, the philosophical position that one takes on this issue affects educationists and drama educationists in particular. The most extreme position is that adopted by the Behaviourist School who have avoided dualism by affirming that what a man is or means is in his behaviour. His mind is an irrelevancy. Teachers therefore are in the business of changing behaviour. In order to change it they have to observe it and measure it. Our fellow drama teachers, particularly in USA who are part of this 'behaviourist system', not surprisingly have adopted a kind of drama that allows the *total* meaning of the drama to be conveyed by the action. They train their students in *theatrical performance*, a mode the sole purpose of which is to make explicit meanings that are not normally communicable. What could be more explicit than the effort made by three young pupils on behalf of their teacher as described in the following extract from a report of the CEMREL Aesthetics Education Experimental Research Project:

> The teacher gave simple instructions to 'listen, watch arms, body etc.' The first three children were sad, happy and surprised in turn. The sad girl rubbed her eyes, commenting 'Oh, I'm so sad'; the happy boy exuberantly jumped up and down and commented 'Oh, I'm so happy. The sun is out.' Later, anger and fright entered the parade. (Smith and Schumacher, 1977, p318)

If we have reservations about the way the behaviourists avoid dualism, we might also have doubts about the way our own Schools Council seem to embrace it. There is more than a hint of a dualistic model operating in the following recommendations:

> Children should become increasingly able to translate attitudes and ideas about various issues into dramatic statements which reflect their understanding. (p144)

> In acting-out children are often given an idea and asked to go away and make something of it, perhaps to arrive at a dramatic statement which encapsulates their feelings and ideas about a particular topic or issue. (p32)

> Acting-out then is the exploration and representation of meaning ... (p16)

> Problems ... may also arise because some children have not clarified their ideas enough to devise a statement about them. (p13) (McGregor *et al*, 1977)

It seems to me from the above statements that we are unambiguously invited to think in terms of an idea in search of a container, as though the two could be conceived of quite separately. This should not distract however from the new emphasis that the authors were introducing: theirs was the first major publication to give priority to *theme* as the principal content of a drama experience. The themes they recommended tend to be of social concern such as 'attitudes to minority groups' or 'the nature of responsibility'. But although the authors firmly espouse the importance of process rather than product, their dualism seems to trap them at times into confining the process to that of finding a theatrical expression for a point of view already held by the participants – searching for a product, no less.

There is an alternative view of process which is worth examining in detail. Drama can be used to *challenge* children's views and understanding, so that although the thematic meaning might still be the nature of responsibility, the drama can be so structured by the teacher that the children are confronted *existentially* by its implications – they experience, for instance, teacher-in-role failing in his responsibility or *vice versa*, so that the outcome is *felt*. But as far as meaning is concerned, it is here we begin to detect the need for making a distinction between 'teacher-meaning' and 'participant-meaning'.

Whereas it might remain legitimate for a teacher to label the thematic meaning as 'the nature of responsibility', when the drama has been of this experiential kind, only in its most reductionist sense could the same label be applied to the participants' experience. That they share this thematic level of meaning is dictated by the structure, but what each child takes from the experience, cognitively and affectively, depends on characteristics uniquely his or her own. Equally important, in answer to the dualist question, the participant is not engaged with the theme or learning area in a compartmentalised way. Plot, contextual and thematic meanings converge not in the Action alone, not in the Mind alone, nor in a sequence of mind and action, but as an integrated whole. The meaning resides in the *person-entering-the-fiction*, and integration of mind and action.

Still less does the notion of theme seem applicable to the experience from the participant's point of view if my definition of theme is adhered to. I wrote that in using the term *theme*, 'a more generalised level of meaning is intended, a higher order of abstraction of human behaviour of which the particular events are an instance'. This is a pretty arid description of an aesthetic event! Arid or not, however, it remains appropriate if we wish to reduce the meaning of an experience to propositional statements. It seems to me that a teacher has little choice. The classification of plot, context and theme is but part of the elaborate epistemological system we have for detaching ourselves from the particularity of experience and as such is necessary if the teacher is to offer herself and others a rationale for his planning. (I am not suggesting that plot, context and theme are the only terminology available to him, but that if he does not use these words he will be obliged to use other conceptualisations.) But because dramatic activity is an art form, it is the very *particularity* of its meaning that counts. The participants do not experience 'responsibility' as an instance of a more general case, but as a unique event not translatable into terms other than itself.

This argument can be pushed further in terms of learning and meaning. Michael Polanyi in a number of texts has discussed different levels of awareness, distinguishing between what he terms subsidiary and focal awareness (see, for example, *Personal knowledge*, Routledge and Kegan Paul, 1958). This has critical implications for the drama teacher for it raises the question of which level of the dramatic activity should have the focus of the participant's attention and which level remains subsidiary (notice that the word 'subsidiary' does not here mean less important – indeed the opposite could apply – but at a lower level of consciousness). It may well be that if the participants enter the fiction with the learning area of 'responsibility' uppermost in their minds then both drama and learning could be unproductive. This point gains further support from some psychologists' acknowledgement that there is a passive, unconscious side to learning processes. In other words it is feasible if not probable that any refinement in understanding of 'responsibility' that occurs during or as a result of the drama experience could be described as 'caught not taught'.

All of which gives credence to the view popularised in recent years that in drama there is often a 'play for the teacher and a play for the pupils'. Whereas the teacher must continue to think and structure in terms of learning area and theme, it is also proper for the participants' focal attention to be directed towards creating a Plot and Context (not, of course, that they will necessarily use these terms in doing so). The teacher's skill, therefore, lies in an ability to set up the drama in a way that ensures a subsidiary awareness of the theme. A further responsibility of the teacher is to set up means for reflection – so that participants can tap for themselves and begin to share with others the meanings that have been implicitly understood.

In *summary* it appears that when the teacher looks for meaning in action only, as, for example, when the story-line or performance modes are stressed, the observer and participant can be said to share the same meaning. Similarly, they can be said to share the same meaning-intention when both teacher and pupil have an abstract theme in mind like 'poverty in the third world' which is to be expressed in a dramatic product. On the other hand, when a teacher alone has a thematic intention which she wants the pupils to *experience* then the principal focus of attention of the participants should, paradoxically, be towards the more superficial goal of using action to meet the demands of plot or context etc. For this kind of drama, observer and participant do not share the same meanings, partly because the participant's experience is unique and partly because he is only subsidiarily aware of the very meanings to which the teacher is giving fullest attention. With this latter point in mind, it may be that Dorothy Heathcote's statement quoted in the first paragraph of this paper should be reversed to read: They must focus on the actions so that the meaning of the drama will come right and true.

Drama in education – a re-appraisal

Drama in education – a reappraisal was first published in McCaslin, N (ed) (1981) Children and drama, 2nd edn., Longman and re-printed in *Gavin Bolton: selected writings.* The title speaks for itself.

An examination of some of the 'myths' that have grown up around drama education

lliott Eisner (1974) some years ago wrote an article challenging the rationale behind many cherished views of art education, assumptions that made up for him a 'mythology' of art education. I shall try to do the same for drama education. There are two points that I need to make before I can start. Exposing a myth is not a denial in absolute terms. One does not argue that something is not valid, but rather that it is only partially valid or that its validity has been misunderstood, misrepresented, distorted or that circumstances have made it less valid. In other words a kernel of truth remains unchallenged. Another point to bear in mind is that just as the creation of a myth is an event in a particular time and a particular place arising out of particular needs, so the erosion of a myth is a particular historical/geographical/philosophical necessity.

Thus this brief study of myths in drama education will apply, and perhaps exclusively, to the English drama scene, both in the myths that were created in the early days of teaching drama to students and in the need in our present educational climate to reappraise our values in drama teaching. For America, past priorities and current challenges to the subject may be of such a different order that this chapter remains but of academic interest to American readers. I hope not. I have a hunch, however, that because of that unchanging kernel of truth within a myth, I am bound to be raising issues of universal importance to drama teachers even though my perspective is necessarily focused (if not blinkered!) by the development of the British educational system.

Myth No. 1: 'Drama is doing'

The sheer relief with which pupils and teachers alike find a salvation from strictures of traditional school studies in the contrasting activity-centred happenings of a drama session is evidence enough, one might have thought, that drama, if it is nothing else, is and indeed must be '*doing*'. Wide disagreement among practitioners as to content, purpose or method can be dispelled in seconds by the common understanding they all share that drama is 'doing'. Nevertheless, I shall argue that this **is** only partially so and that it is the neglect of the part that is *not* 'doing' that has distorted our understanding of the nature of drama and has caused us to underrate its potential for learning.

Of course the critical characteristic of drama is concrete action: it is this that distinguishes it from other arts, even from its sister arts of movement and dance, which, also action bound, nevertheless are spatially and temporarily more abstract. It is not, however, the concrete action alone that carries the meaning of the experience. Indeed I shall attempt to show that the meaning of a dramatic experience is not so much bound up with the functional, imitative meaning of the action, as with a tension that is set up between the particularity of the action and the generality of meanings implied by the action. The meaning of the experience is both dependent on and independent of the concrete action.

Action, even imitative action, is not in itself drama. A child miming the action of posting a letter is not in a dramatic mode if his sole intention is accurately to imitate such an action. He is merely adopting an imitative mode of behaviour, selecting an activity, the meaning of which can be denoted by the terms 'posting a letter' and recalling in imitative actions precisely that function. There is but one dimension of meaning represented by the imitation: the denotative or functional one.

For the action to be considered dramatic greater significance of meaning must lie along other dimensions. (Sadly, many Drama Education 'packages' seem to rely heavily on the one dimension of imitation, even to imitating *emotions!*) Such significance is determined by the combination of two contrasting sources: whatever is uniquely personal and whatever is more universally relevant. Thus posting a letter as dramatic action must arouse affective memories in the participant to do with posting letters sufficiently strong for the action significantly to feed into appropriate meanings such as 'trust in a written message', 'irrevocability of a decision to post a letter', 'the anticipation of a letter's impact' and 'the impotence of not knowing the receiver's reaction'. It is these connotations that go beyond the functional meaning that the participant in drama must be concerned with. It is in this sense therefore that one can say the meaning of the dramatic experience is independent of the action. On the other hand the action of posting a letter is the vehicle through which such connotations are expressed. In that sense, therefore, the meaning is dependent on the concrete action. Thus the overall meaning is expressed in a relationship between the particular action and its more universal implications. Those teachers who are content to train their students in imitative skills are off target – imitating human actions and emotions is not drama. Likewise those teachers who, in their anxiety for students to achieve significantly thoughtful work, neglect the potential power of the concrete action do so at their peril – for the handling of abstract ideas, even in role, without some spatial/temporal reference is not in itself drama either.

In England we have large numbers of the former teachers who see the training of students in skilful miming actions as sufficient drama training. It is to these teachers one has to exclaim 'drama is *not* doing!' whereas to the latter teachers, often found among teachers in the humanities who see the educational opportunities in holding discussions on some important issues in role, one says 'this is really an abstract exchange of views which is fine as far as it goes, but drama is doing!' I hope my arguments have been sufficiently clear for the reader to appreciate that both forms of advice are misleading. Perhaps we should say 'drama is/is not doing'. Only with her sights ambivalently adjusted is a teacher likely to gauge correctly her priorities in teaching drama. We do not wish to limit our students to learning more precisely the functional actions of life: it is the significance of the universal implication behind those actions that learning in drama is concerned with. In attempting to challenge the myth of 'drama is doing' therefore, I am not merely clarifying the nature of drama but, more importantly, showing that a teacher's priorities must inevitably become adjusted when its nature is properly grasped.

Myth No. 2: 'Drama is an escape from reality'

Some play theorists see the make-believe play of young children as compensating for the 'slings and arrows of outrageous fortune,' as the child's natural means of protecting herself from the cruel realities of living. Because drama is undoubtedly linked with play (perhaps another 'myth' is that drama *is* play!) some practitioners see drama as an outlet for their students, either in the sense of 'letting off steam' or as an opportunity to fantasise. The former describes a psychological disposition; the latter is concerned with drama's content. I shall discuss these in turn starting with the content.

a) The content of drama

To view make-believe activity as an escape from reality is, it seems to me, to ignore a critical attribute of both play and drama: the child at play, far from evading restrictions, actually imposes them. As the Russian psychologist, Vygotsky (1976) has pointed out, play is about abiding by the rules. The same applies to drama. However 'unreal' the make-believe situation may be, the rules themselves objectively reflect the real world, even if it is an inverse re-flection: if, for example, the rule is, to choose an extreme example, 'all parents have to be punished and sent to bed early by their children' this merely (not merely – significantly perhaps) reflects a very clear acknowledgement of reality, as does every piece of apparent fantasy. But a feature of play is that a child may give up playing or just change the rules when he feels so inclined. Drama, on the other hand, requires students to agree on the rules, acknow-ledge their parameters and keep to them, *even when it becomes uncomfort-able.*

It so often happens that children choose a topic they do not fully understand and when they begin to perceive its implications subtly start to undermine the rules that are implicit in the situation. In other words, instead of facing up to the rigour of thinking, decision making and coping with tension inherent within a topic, they prefer to slacken their grip on 'the rules of the game'. Thus it is in this sense that drama can be an escape from reality, where an unspoken concensus between class and teacher allows a drifting into a 'rule-less' activity – immediately gratifying, eventually frustrating, educationally poverty stricken. I can think of many examples: of a class of nine year olds who in choosing to do their drama about hijacking sought 'fantasy' ways of solving the problem of being in the hijacker's power, by suddenly producing weapons (one boy tried claiming magic power!) they had clearly not had in their pos-session when the hijack first took place. At an adult level, I recall a woman who in playing a role of a singleminded determined person, under pressure from other people in the improvisation, 'succumbed' in a way that was quite illogi-cal for the character she was playing.

On the other hand, I also recall as teacher of a class of 10-11 year olds over-insisting on keeping to historical facts. The situation was about Florence Nightingale and her nurses who were sent out by Queen Victoria to tend to the many wounded in the military hospital at Scutari, only to find on arrival that the doctors running the hospital were refusing to allow women on the wards. 'Nursing is a man's job' they firmly declared. Now the boys and girls in this class representing the doctors and nurses respectively explored many of the facets of this confrontation during four or five drama sessions, the girls successively adapting their tactics along a wide range of ploys from demands to requests, from blackmail to persuasion. By the fifth day the doctors went into private conclave and eventually whispered to me that they were going to offer a compromise: the nurses were to be given a chance to work on the wards for just one day – to prove themselves! I am sure the reader will agree that this was a mature decision for young children to take. Unfortunately, in my enthusiasm for historical facts, I would not let them do this – for historically the doctors did not give in in that way. (For those readers who are interested, the doctors at Scutari capitulated, not from choice, but because after a particularly severe battle, there were more wounded than the male orderlies and doctors could cope with.) Even as I write I shudder at the harm that some of us as teachers do! It is quite obvious that I as a teacher was allowing myself to be controlled by a very limited kind of reality – a particular sequence of events – whereas the more important reality was to do with how people adjust to an *impasse.*

What the boys wanted to carry out was *objectively valid,* in so far as they had examined the various factors in the situation and made a reasoned judgement about them. This then is what is meant by the relationship of drama to reality – it is the perception, recognition and appraisal of events within the fictitious context. The context may be close to a known social context or an apparent fantasy, but it is the rules that govern it that must reflect the objective world for the activity to be worthy of the term drama and worthy of education.

Disposition towards drama

What people usually mean by 'letting off steam' is a psychological release from tension, so that participants are supposed to 'feel better' after a drama experience. This represents a pretty crude view of the mental state of drama participants, but there is a more subtle expectation of our students' mental state that was first conceived in England by the great pioneer of child drama, Peter Slade (1954) and taken up staunchly by his disciples ever since. I refer to the quality of *absorption.*

It may puzzle the reader that I should include this admirable quality which most of us as teachers have at one time or another worked to promote in our students among the 'myths' of drama in education. I shall not argue that it is mythical in the sense that it doesn't exist (although some teachers working continually with recalcitrant classes may sometimes wonder!) but that we have been wrong to see it as a final achievement. Indeed I used to assume that if my students were absorbed then that was a necessary and sufficient concomitant of learning.

But I want to suggest that this may not be the case: that there is something about 'absorption' which hints at 'being lost' in an experience, thus escaping from reality. Now I know that the look of wonder on a child's face when he is so 'lost' can be something to be marvelled at, but I do not think it is moments such as these that we are working for in drama. We do not want children to 'lose' themselves but '*find*' themselves.

Certainly we want a high degree of involvement and commitment to the creative fiction, but if it is to be a worthwhile learning experience for the participant he must hold a dual perspective on the experience: an active identification with the fiction combined with heightened awareness of his own identification. So, far from escaping from life, the quality of life is momentarily intensified because he is 'knowing what he thinks as he thinks it'; 'seeing what he says as he says it'; 'evaluating what he does as he does it'. It is this reflection concurrent with identification that leads to learning through drama. Sometimes, of course, students are not capable of so reflecting. It is then that the teacher having attempted to discern what it is the student has experienced can perhaps, after the drama, help him to retrace the experience and reflect upon it or, alternatively, can attempt to create a frame of mind in the student that will bring about a more heightened awareness when he enters the next phase of the drama. With such sensitive handling by the teacher the student can begin to use fiction to understand himself in the real world.

Myth No. 3: 'Drama education is concerned with developing the uniqueness of the individual'

It is not insignificant I think that at the time Winifred Ward was establishing the term 'Creative dramatics' in America, here in England our Peter Slade was introducing the label 'Child drama'.

The latter terminology was intended to imply that within each child there is a potential for dramatic expression that is important because it is personal. The teacher's responsibility lay in nurturing a person's individuality. Such a philosophical view of the child and of drama as being 'within him' should be seen as part of a larger educational trend in Europe beginning with Rousseau, through Froebel and Pestalozzi and culminating in our own Plowden Report in 1967, which gave a seemingly final official stamp of approval to 'child-centred education'. It is perhaps true to say that whereas the 'humanist movement' in America has been a counter movement to the application of behaviourism to education, the 'child-centred' movement in England was seen as an alternative to the persistent image of children as passive recipients of an approved body of knowledge. It is not surprising when the child-centred movement was in the ascendancy in the 1950s and 60s that personalities in drama education should emerge to pioneer a view of drama that was also child-centred. The message of drama as personal development was welcomed hungrily not only in England but throughout the Western world for it bravely stood up to both the 'body of knowledge' and the 'behaviourist' explications of education. Drama teachers were grateful to Brian Way (1967) in particular for articulating a philosophy that emphasised the *process* of dramatic experience rather than the *product*, that saw drama as a means of approach to self-knowledge and even (as taken further by devotees like Richard Courtney) as the very basis of all the learning and growth – *Developmental* drama was the Courtney label that spread through Canada.

In England our interpretation of Brian Way's philosophy tended to be manifested by our concern with the importance of individual creativity and free expression often paradoxically catered for in practice by exercise sequences for disciplined attributes like concentration or the puppet like response to a signal from teacher's tambour; with a growing hostility to the notion of children performing; with the assumption that there can be no sense of standards in drama work because each child is his own arbiter in this respect; and with the claim that 'Drama is Life' thus effectively reducing the activity to a meaningless catch-phrase.

But there is one aspect, our concern with promoting the uniqueness of the individual that perhaps more than the other manifestations goes in my view against the natural dramatic grain. There are some art forms, painting in particular, that are a vehicle for individual expression, but drama by its very nature is a group statement, commenting on, exploring, questioning or celebrating not individual differences, but what man has in common with man.

I have already mentioned different levels of meaning in dramatic action. In the example of posting a letter I suggested there are three broad levels of meaning – the functional (the imitative action of posting a letter), the universal (significant implications that posting a letter might have such as the irretrievability of the action) and the personal (whatever 'posting letter' memories a particular child may recall). Now each of these levels of meaning is important for the total meaning of the experience is made up of their interaction. But for the activity to be drama and not solitary play the concentration of effort must be at the middle level of meaning, that is it must have some significance related to the concrete action that all the participants can share. If the context or plot of the drama with six year olds is, for example, to do with 'catching a monster' the 'shared' or 'thematic' meaning might be 'we dare not make a mistake' or 'it is important to distinguish between 'evidence' and 'rumour' of the monster's existence' or 'are we to be destroyers or preservers of life?' With ten year olds whose dramatic context is space travel the theme might well be 'Is our training good enough for what we have to face?' or 'having to make a decision based on inadequate knowledge' or 'the responsibility we have to all those who will follow'. A group of sixteen year olds might be looking at 'family' contexts where the theme might be 'the dependence/ independence ambivalence of the different generations', 'the treasure/ burden ambivalence of rearing a child' or 'a family as a symbol of a past and a future'.

Of course each individual will bring all kinds of personal meanings to the above dramas, some more relevant than others. Indeed they could vary from traumatic for the six year old who is scared at the very thought of monsters or for the sixteen year old whose family is breaking up, to the neutral feelings of the six year old whose mind is really on his new birthday presents or to the positively destructive attitude of a sixteen year old who is hostile to drama. But if the experience is to operate as *drama*, individual differences must be channelled into the collective theme. Ultimately, however, it is what the individual draws from the collective meaning that matters, a process of 'finding himself in the meaning'. In that sense the importance of the uniqueness of the individual is not a myth, but like a member of an audience the individual has temporarily to hold his individuality in abeyance, sharing meanings he has in common with others in order that he may be personally enriched.

Myth No. 4: Drama is personal development

I do not wish to deny that drama, along with all aspects of education, can be an aid to personal development. Indeed I think I could argue the case that drama more than other subjects of the curriculum may accelerate the maturing process, especially for those children who for some reason or other have had natural progress arrested. Why then have I placed drama as personal development among my list of myths? The reason lies within our past reluctance to distinguish between immediate educational objectives and long-term maturation. Enthusiasm for the personal development of their students has often led to an act of super-arrogation on the part of drama teachers who claim that personal development is what they were actually *teaching*. One cannot *teach* concentration, trust, sensitivity, group awareness, patience, tolerance, respect, perception, judgement, social concern, coping with ambivalent feelings, responsibility etc, etc; one can only hope that education will help to bring them about over a long term and as I have already suggested it could be argued that drama brings them about in a special way, but the achievement of these admirable qualities is *not intrinsic to drama*: it is an important *by-product* of the dramatic experience.

Certainly a teacher can effectively structure to create opportunities for continual practice of many of the above attributes but the drama must itself be *about* something. Sadly, it has so often been relegated to dramatic exercise in personal skills, just as in the old days poetry used to be abused in its usage as a mere vehicle for speech practice.

Among the many immediate objectives a teacher may have for a particular drama lesson or series of lessons extending the students' understanding of the thematic content must be a top priority. Other objectives such as effective use of the art form and satisfaction from a sense of achievement follow closely. Now it seems to me that the students' regular opportunity for exploration of meanings within a theme through the effective use of the art form can cumulatively provide the very processes that will bring about trust, sensitivity, concentration and the rest. But the teacher's and students' immediate concern must be with *meaning*. In England we have trained a whole generation of drama teachers to whom this would be a novel suggestion – drama lessons for them have been but a series of varied dramatic exercises that purport to train the students in life-skills.

Myth No. 5: Drama is anti-theatre

The relationship between theatre and drama is a complex one, the subtleties of which have been virtually ignored in the UK because of the historical situation which drove drama teachers into two opposite camps – those who saw school drama as the acquisition of theatre skills, training students as performers and those who believed in child-centred education, the 'progressiveness' of which was measured by the degree to which the students were not trained as performers. The latter claimed that the educational reward came from the dramatic process, not its product.

Although the position I take on this is that the greater potential educational value lies in students' *experiencing* drama rather than *performing* it, I nevertheless regret that polarisation into an either/or situation has occurred. It is not that I feel uncomfortable faced with alternative philosophies in education; I have no wish to martial everyone into the same camp. My regret stems from something much more fundamental: that teachers have not been given a sufficient conceptual basis from which to make a reasoned choice between the two.

I propose to examine what I see as essential differences and similarities between drama and theatre in respect of *mode* and *structure*: other aspects, for instance, that theatre is normally linked with a *place* and that for many people theatre is a *job* I shall not discuss here.

Mode

By mode I am referring to the quality of the behaviour of any participant who is consciously engaged in some form of make-believe activity. If we were to watch a child in a garden being a policeman, we would say he is 'playing'; if we watched an actor on stage being a policeman, we would say he is 'performing'. We might agree that although both are 'pretending' there is a difference in *quality* or *mode* of action. It will be useful here to attempt to determine at least some of the characteristics of these two behaviours. You will notice I have called them 'playing' and 'performing', apparently avoiding the term 'acting'. At the risk of offending those readers who have a very clearly defined notion of acting as something only an actor does, I intend to use the term as all-embracing, applying it to both the child's and the adult's behaviour. This allows me to think in terms of *continuum* of acting behaviour rather than two separate categories:

Acting

Dramatic Playing ◀━━━━━━━━━▶ Performing

I have changed the terminology at the left end of the continuum to '*dramatic playing*' rather than just playing – this is to distinguish it from much child play that does not involve make-believe or pretence – such as ball playing. I am now in a position to argue that the *mode* changes according to which end of the continuum the acting behaviour orientates.

Let us look at the extreme left end first. It is not easy to find the words adequately to describe a child absorbed in dramatic playing: 'being' or 'experiencing' might well convey the right qualities. It seems to be both active and passive in the sense that the child is responsible for his own playing and yet is at the same time submitting to the effect of his own contriving. Thus he could say 'I am making it happen, so that it can happen to me' and he could add 'and it is happening to me *now*'. Thus the experiential mode of dramatic playing can be distinguished by (1) both a deliberate devising and a spontaneous responding, (2) a sense of 'nowness' and (3) ME in the experience. If we take our child playing a policeman the three features are demonstrated as follows: (1) In order to give himself a 'policeman' experience he must contrive to recall and imitate 'policeman-like' activities, at least, as we have discussed earlier, in so far as they are relevant to the *personal* meaning he is exploring. (2) He must achieve a sense of 'policeman' things happening to him as he plays, for example visualising that traffic is *now* whirling round him under his control and (3) the experience, while ostensibly about 'policeman', is really about him in a 'policeman' context.

I have discussed earlier the 'heightened awareness' that increases the chances of a child's reflecting upon and learning from the experience. A feature of this awareness that is relevant here is that whereas a child can say 'It is happening to me now' she also knows it is fiction. This paradox that it is happening and yet not happening ('psychical distancing', a term employed by Bullough (1912) in relation to audience attitude in particular, might be appropriate here) provides us with a fourth essential characteristic of the mode of a child's dramatic playing.

Now if we move to the extreme right of our continuum, it becomes clear that all four features, contriving responding, sense of 'nowness', sense of 'me-ness' and psychical distancing, although essentially present for the actor are significantly reduced or over-shadowed by a new set of intentions to do with interpretation, character portrayal, repeatability, projection, communicability and empathy with an audience. Heightened awareness, not to mention entertainment, must ultimately be enjoyed by the *audience*. Child drama, creative drama, creative dramatics, educational drama, whatever we care to call non-performance drama in schools seems logically to be placed towards the left rather than the right of the continuum for the ultimate responsibility, intention and skills of the actor must lie in his ability to give someone else an experience. In other words the fundamental difference in the *mode* required lies not just in the skills employed but is a matter of *mental set*. This difference seems to be so decisive that one might wonder whether indeed the notion of a continuum should be scrapped and replaced by distinct categories, thus validating the anti-theatre attitude among drama educationalists, a view that in practice one sees painfully reinforced by those many occasions in schools where young children are directed into a totally inappropriate mental set of taking responsibility for entertaining adults. The harm in my view lies not just in demands made on the children by the particular occasion itself, but in the subsequent attitude of those children who, feeling inadequate, are put off drama by the experience or those who, finding a flair in themselves for entertaining, continue to view drama as an opportunity for furthering facile techniques, which teachers, also unfortunately deceiving themselves, persist in encouraging.

Nevertheless, in spite of evidence of some appalling examples of children thrust into harmful theatre experiences, in spite of the distinction that logically can be sustained of alternative mental sets, I now propose to argue that there are enough occasions in children's play, student's creative drama and theatrical performance when the acting mode in terms of the participant's intention of mental set is ambiguous and not purely one thing or another to justify the image of a continuum rather than separate categories.

There are a number of instances when child play, dramatic activity and performance seem to shift their position along the mode continuum. I propose to list some examples of these.

Child play

Sometimes a child playing on his own, absorbed in make-believe – let us take our 'policeman' example – will say to his mother when she enters, 'Look Mummy, I am a policeman'. Now this implies not only a shift in intention (he was up to that point doing the actions for himself only) but a possible change in meaning. For whatever *subjective* meanings the 'policeman' action expressed may now be held in abeyance for the sake of communication. Just as language has a private and public function, so *action* has both connotative and denotative functions. Although to a hidden observer the child may be repeating the same 'policeman' actions, it might well be only the public functional meaning that the child is now interested in sharing with his mother. This does not of course become a theatrical performance, for the actor's responsibility is to make sure the audience identify with all levels of meaning.[1] But the point I want to make is that using fictitious action for the sake of communication to someone else can start early on in child behaviour. To put it another way, a change of some kind in the quality or mode is well within the capacity of a child, even a young one.

Dramatic activity

We rightly claim that students in 'experiencing' drama are not concerned with communicating to an audience. And yet this does seem to ignore three features:

1   That they often as they participate adapt the quality of the mode in order to communicate a variety of levels to each other.
2   That the use of constant intervention by teacher, in inviting them to reflect on what they have just done or are about to do, also invites them to see their work very much as a series of products to be evaluated rather than a process to be left undisturbed.

3   In spite of the concentration on 'experiencing', when the quality of work is aesthetically satisfying to the participant, the many layers of meaning communicate themselves to an observer *even when there is no intention so to communicate.*

I think the above three points sufficiently illustrate that within the process of experiencing with its overall orientation towards the left of the continuum there appear to be contrary pulls in the other direction. Similarly, when we now look at 'performance' we can detect a less rigid position.

Performance

The obvious examples of a different orientation:

1   Those times in rehearsal when an actor is drawing on his own re-sources to find meaning are very close to what a child goes through in a drama experience.

2   Those performances where spontaneity of interaction among the per-formers themselves is deliberately kept alive so that fresh meanings can emerge for the actors. In other words the actors are operating at a double level of both communicating pre-conceived meanings and at the same time generating (actually experiencing as in drama) new meanings.

I hope I have established that in terms of quality or mode of acting the form of behaviour that one might expect of a child at play, a student drama and an actor in theatre has at times sufficient in common at least to blur the edges of distinctions between them. Let us now examine the drama/theatre dicho-tomy in terms of form.

Form

It is when we examine drama and theatre form that we find not just similarity but a considerable overlap, enough to justify the argument that structurally drama and theatre are indistinguishable. The basic elements of both are focus, tension, contrast and symbolisation. It seems to me that just as a play-wright working for theatre is concerned with using these elements to convey his meaning, so a teacher working in creative drama is concerned with helping students to explore meaning through the use of these same elements. So in a curious way when even young children are working in creative dramatics they are working in a theatre form and the teacher's function can be seen as an extension of a playwright, sharpening and deepening that form.

Let me now summarise this long section on the relations between drama and theatre. I have claimed that one of the myths about drama is that it is anti-theatre. Even as I write this I am aware this is a dangerous thing to say for people will assume I want a return to the old 'train children to perform' days, so let me first spell out what I do *not* mean:

I do *not* want drama to be seen as training in acting techniques.

I do *not* want to encourage large-scale spectacular productions of the kind that require the teacher/director to be brilliantly inventive and the performers to be conforming automatons (unfortunately such presentations can be so impressively polished and slick and the loud prolonged applause can convince parents, education officials, teachers – and, of course, the treasurer – that they must be of educational value).

But, on the other hand, I am convinced there are firmer connections between drama and theatre than we have in the past acknowledged, subtle connections which, if more understood, would allow us to *harness* the notion of 'showing' drama instead of either despising it or using it superficially. Different kinds of performing, varying in the degree to which they are formal/informal, audience oriented/audience ignored, finished product/lasting a few seconds, a script interpretation/a group's dramatic statement, a collage of scripted excerpts/a whole play. Whichever of these dimensions is selected the potential pivotal relationship between 'experiencing' and 'showing' which we have tended to ignore can occasionally sharpen the work at the dramatic playing end of the continuum and always enrich any move towards the other end.

Final comment

In this chapter I have outlined what might be called the 'mythology' of drama education. The 'myths' I have selected are 'Drama is doing', 'Drama is an escape from reality', 'Drama is concerned with the uniqueness of the individual', 'Drama is for personal development', 'Drama is anti-theatre'. Having argued against all these I perhaps need to remind readers what I said at the beginning, that in important ways they *are* viable: drama in a narrow sense *is* doing; drama for some children can be used as an escape from a reality that is painful to them; drama education is ultimately of course, concerned with the uniqueness of the individual and his personal development and drama although not anti-theatre does offer critical differences of emphasis that are ignored at our peril.

My aim therefore has been to extend the conceptual framework so that we have a firmer basis from which to examine these important issues.

Note

1 It is relevant to refer here to the form of drama, popular particularly in our secondary schools, where students are required to improvise in their groups 'making up' a play to show the others at the end of the session. In such circumstances the teachers, unwittingly, may be inviting the students merely to prepare the *denotative* meanings for the sake of easy communication.

IN DEFENCE OF DRAMA IN EDUCATION

Drama in education:
learning medium or arts process?

The occasion for the reading of this paper (1982) was the second of a series of major annual conferences inaugurated by the National Association for the Teaching of Drama. The first address, given the year before, had been published as 'Heathcote at the National'. It was part of a developing war of words that was starting to emerge with David Hornbrook, Malcolm Ross, Robert Witkin (see Introduction) and even John Fines, who was firmly in the Heathcote camp (see below), shooting across the bows of the drama in education world. Gavin Bolton was the key defender of drama in education as both a learning medium and an art form.

Things are happening in the drama educational world. The alarm is being sounded. A call to arms! The battle cry can be heard from Chichester to Exeter. Forces are gathering; manoeuvres are under way. At last a bit of excitement. After all these dreary years of Schools Council eclecticism and blandness, people are taking sides, declaring loyalties, waving banners. And somewhere in the middle of the battlefield, trying to run hard to get out of the way but not sure which way to run for safety is *me*. But swords are not very sharp and the war cries are perhaps not so much a threat as an invitation to join the ranks. However, I want to stay where I am, and this paper is to be a justification for trying to be loyal to both camps at the same time while denying the prerogative of one over the other. Let me paint the scene of battle.

John Fines, in addressing a group of teacher-trainers in September, speaking with a strength of conviction that sent them all scribbling in their note-books, pronounced, "As-if' is possible wherever you go in education, and ...', he added with a 'mock' cutting glance in my direction, 'you do not have to put the word *drama* in it'. As an historian who has discovered the 'as-if' game can be played successfully in the classroom when the teacher wants children to get to grips with people's attitudes behind historical events, Dr Fines with his colleague Ray Verrier (Fines and Verrier, 1974), has made a strong case for the use of 'dramatic method'. He knows that the educational value of his method is unchallengeable and is both astonished and disapproving of the move I have been making in recent years towards emphasising the importance of dramatic form. He certainly thinks that my attempt to analyse form is a waste of time. And he would be shocked at my recent recommendation that all teachers of drama should be trained in theatre arts.

But it has been my turn to be astonished. As a postscript to a paper I read at an Exeter conference on aesthetics last summer, Malcolm Ross (1982) seems to be holding me responsible for all that's wrong with drama. He condemns my practical work on the grounds that it is overemotional, manipulative, thematically-centred and anti-theatre. In respect of the latter he writes:

> Many drama teachers take their lessons and inspiration from the theatre (the writings of Brook and Grotowski for example) rather than from educational sources – and with drama in education in such difficulties they'd probably be right to go on doing so. It's certainly high time the wrangle between theatre and drama was wound up. Drama in education is a doomed mutant unless it can draw life from the theatre. (p152)

It is difficult to grasp how Malcolm Ross can argue the above point in opposition to my paper which includes the following assertion:

> The history of drama in education in this country had polarised between the two camps, between what was called 'creative' or 'child' drama and 'performance' ... It seems to me that these factions, in emphasising differences at a peripheral level of skills, are failing to recognise the common ground between them. Indeed I would like to argue that most drama teachers of whatever persuasion are at a fundamental level using the same dramatic form. The 'clay' of drama is the same for the teacher, the pupil, the playwright, the director and the actor ... Regrettably we do not train our teachers to know the basic feel of that clay and yet this is what they should be passing on to their pupils – the essence of dramatic form. (*ibid*, p142)

Does this really seem that I am anti-theatre? But he also suggests that I am manipulative (yes I agree and I have never claimed otherwise), too concerned with issues and themes (I would have thought I am in good company here – many playwrights and directors share such a concern) and that my work invites emotionally reactive (to use his terminology) rather than reflexive behaviour (I need to answer this one at length) and also that I work at the wrong pace! Let us look further at what he says:

> I feel drama in education is often too dominated by concern with themes and topics to the neglect of medium control; is too extravagant and excitable, often on account of some commitment by the drama teacher to giving the children a good (i.e. 'hot') time in every single lesson ... Drama in my view needs to be much cooler, and the work much more respectful of the intensely complex nature of the medium. It needs to run more slowly and temperately. (*ibid*, p149)

I never thought the day would come when I could be accused of working too fast! It is ironical that the most common complaint I receive from teachers is that they bite their finger nails down to the quick in their frustration at the diffident, exploratory, reflective *legato* of my work with children. They have also often expressed exasperated concern at the lack of excitement in the work. Indeed, taking the sensation out of what appears to be a sensational topic is one of the things I might be considered to be good at! For many years my concern has been to help children find awe in the ordinary.

So does Malcolm Ross know anything at all about my work and the kind of educational drama I stand for? I cannot think that if he has come into contact with it he has understood it. And yet he does have before him the paper I read in which I described a class of fourteen year old Manchester boys choosing the topic of 'the city of Manchester preparing for a nuclear holocaust' which, in terms of 'ordinariness' centred on things like 'how deep will the air-raid shelter have to be?' and the victims of radiation years later being spoon-fed by a nurse. Malcolm Ross, in his postscript also gives a practical illustration from his own teaching, showing us how drama *ought* to be handled. He works with a group of two, making the point that three people, two participants and an observer, make an ideal grouping. I cannot think, however, that his particular example helps him to make the contrast with my work that he wishes to underline. For he exercises the teacher's right as manipulator by offering the group a script (*Dr Faustus*). And the central idea of the work, using the Helen of Troy scene, revolves round the notion of 'intercourse with the dead' (his words). Is this not a *theme* and is not intercourse with the dead a wee bit *sensational*?

But no doubt he would argue that whereas his group's work was emotionally cool, mine was not. He seems to be able to detect that whereas in my work the participants have emotions which are bad, in his work they have something much superior – *feelings* which are, of course, good. To use his terminology my classes respond reactively, his reflexively. I have looked up what he means by reactive behaviour. In his book, *The creative arts* (1978), he gives a list of examples of such behaviour:

> Reactive expression releases energy. Reactive expression serves to reduce an uncomfortable state of arousal to a more tolerable level. We all respond reactively to situations, to frustrations, anger, anxiety, disappointment, fear, sudden surprise. We lash out physically and verbally, we run away, we run amok, we gasp, we groan, we roar with delight or rage, we flash our eyes, raise our voice, wring our hands, hide the face we have lost or are in danger of losing. (p41)

Is this what Ross thinks goes on in my lessons? But the theory he has bound himself to does not seem to recognise the importance of any kind of spontaneous emotional response. I would like to know how in his session on *Faustus* he managed to avoid it for it seems to me that far from avoiding it he *used* it. Before the group of three worked on the text they 'doodled' using their bodies experimentally in space. He explains as follows:

> I watched and listened and helped them select what turned out to be the 'holding form' for the rest of the day's work. This was a simple encounter situation in which the girl moved towards the man who prepared to embrace her only to find her walk on 'through' the embrace. The event occurred fortuitously and was selected from much else on the grounds that both actors and observer sensed its dramatic quality and possibilities. (p151)

I would like to know how they can 'fortuitously' experience a thwarted embrace without an emotional response of something like frustration, embarrassment or amusement. It seems to me that such fortuitous occurrences give a drama lesson its richness. It is the excitement of that shared moment that can be harnessed and recaptured when they turn to the text – surely a process of working in drama that we learnt at our mother's knee. Why does Malcolm Ross need to try to establish his method as an alternative way of working? Any teacher who has an enlightened approach will use this among many approaches.

I find a lot of what he has to say just balderdash. Which is a pity, because underneath it all I have some respect for what Malcolm is trying to say. John Fines, who does know my work well, its strengths and its weaknesses, has expressed alarm because he is afraid I am in danger of identifying too closely with the Ross-type philosophy of arts education. I can respect John Fines' challenge and wish to take it seriously. I want to take Malcolm Ross seriously, but I think I feel insulted by his post-script to my paper because he has chosen to ignore one of the threads of my argument which was to point out that in drama in school (and here I am quoting from the last line of my paper): 'At its most profound, through the art form, our deepest levels may be touched as we engage with what is outside ourselves' (*ibid*, p147). Indeed, you would not know from Ross's criticism of my paper that for most of it I was attempting to establish the importance of dramatic form. What he does not like, of course, is that I also state quite categorically that for me good education is what I am interested in first and foremost. Whether it is conceivable to see art and learning as compatible is something I propose to take up now.

This is a huge topic and because so much of the Ross postscript is concerned with quality of feeling, I have decided to look at the relation between Art and Learning through the particular focus of Emotion. I shall outline a model which challenges Ross's theory not by finding some logical flaw in it – I am not good at that – but by posing an alternative model which draws heavily on what I see happens when children participate in drama. I cannot offer it as evidence only as a hypothesis.

One of Ross's major worries has been that drama in schools operates at an excitement level which can at best be unproductive. (It is a pity, I think, that the only drama lesson described by Robert Witkin in *Intelligence of feeling* (1974) was one that got out of hand.) However, I wish to argue that built in to the dramatic mode are a number of safety valves which are worthy of our detailed attention.

I have for some years now been gnawing at the notion of distinct kinds of acting behaviour and on my visit to Australia three years ago I tried out a paper rather weirdly titled 'Emotion in the dramatic process – is it an adjective or a verb?' (1978) (I have not been invited back to Australia!) Only recently have I come across – or rather, it would be more accurate to say that Ken Robinson (1981) put me in the direction of an author, Alan Tormey (1971), who also uses a grammatical analogy, and although he is a philosopher he uses a number of references to the acting process in order to illumine his elegantly argued thesis on the nature of *expression*. His thesis is that there is a double valence to behaviour – expressive behaviour *and* representational behaviour. Expressive behaviour implies a state of emotional arousal; representational behaviour does not – it merely 'detaches the surface of expressive behaviour'. Both are present in the actor simultaneously.

Before adapting his thesis to my own ends I need to explain what he means by expression. As I intend to make it the very basis of my dramatic model, we need to understand the precise way in which it is being used. Expressive behaviour is verbal or non-verbal. It points simultaneously in two directions: towards some state of emotional arousal in the person (say, anger or wonder or pleasure); and towards what he calls an intentional object, something outside the person to which the state of arousal is prepositionally related. (I am angry *over* an act of injustice or I wonder *at* the sight of Niagara Falls or I am pleased *with* my garden). We might well be inclined to call this intentional object the *context* of the emotional arousal for it is the cognitive relationship with a particular context that gives the emotion its particular characteristics. There is really no such experience of an emotion called anger – there is only my anger, in *this* context, on *this* particular occasion. Notice also the expressive behaviour in this definition does not distinguish voluntary and involuntary behaviour. If I blush with embarrassment at being caught in a lie, my response is just as expressive as if I complain to a neighbour about a noisy dog. Both entail a subjective-objective relationship. Expressive behaviours then by this definition are very common occurring from minute to minute within our day.

Now a further dimension which is critical to this thesis, is the *mode of the* expression. This will obviously vary according to whether what is occurring is entirely for oneself (subjective) or whether it involves someone else. Angrily banging the door to when my son has left it open for the umpteenth time is different from complaining to him about it over lunch. Both are expressive, but quite different in form. On the other hand the action of banging that door to can itself have two importantly distinct orientations. If I angrily bang that door long after my son has departed, the experience is one kind of expression, but if I were to bang it knowing full well he would hear it, that is a different mode of expression. Although the action is the same the *intention* is different.

A few weeks ago my wife and I were leaning over a parapet looking onto a jetty where a deep-sea diver was getting into his skins in order to untangle some rope which had got caught underneath a moored vessel due to depart. The diver had obviously been 'called in' to solve the problem. He looked none too happy and gave a great sigh. A moment or so later he suddenly caught sight of us watching – and he gave another great sigh. But this one was different, for having been absorbed in what he was doing, he suddenly saw himself as an *object* of our attention. He responded accordingly and 'placed' his sigh in our direction. It was a calculated, 'public' action, a 'depicted' or 'performed' sigh. He had moved from subjectively experiencing to objectively representing. I do not know whether it was the 'same' sigh in physical terms, whether for instance it involved the same volume of breath exhalation, but I do know that the intention and effort and therefore the *meaning* had changed. I want to suggest that whereas the spontaneous, private first sigh was *occurring*, the second calculated public sigh was descriptive. The first was expressive of his state of experiencing, to use a grammatical analogy, a verb; the second was *descriptive* of his state of experiencing, an adjective. The first was fluid and not easy to recapture; the second was static, conventional and accessible to repetition.

Was the second sigh phony? In one way it was not because it represented a state of feeling that he was actually experiencing, but there nevertheless was an element of deception in that he was pretending the sigh was spontaneous, experiential, subjective. It was in fact adjectival – demonstrating *how* he felt – but he wanted us to believe in it as a verb, a spontaneous occurrence. It was an instance of contrived spontaneity. When I bang the door in my son's hearing, it may be purely subjective because I am oblivious he is there; on the other hand I may be doing it knowing he is there and in all honesty demonstrating my anger to him; I may, however, intend to demonstrate but want him to believe it was my subjective reaction, as if I did not realise he was there – thus another example of contrived spontaneity. Only in acting is contrived spontaneity legitimised and seen as having integrity.

The actor offers us the adjective – and we, the audience, see the action as a verb, as someone's experiencing. But it is the character's verb, not the actor's, for dramatic behaviour is holding two worlds in one's head at the same time, what Augusto Boal (1981) calls '*metaxis*', a continual change of state, a dialectic between the actual and the fictitious. In actuality the actor adopts the demonstrating or describing mode, but he portrays or depicts the character's spontaneous experiencing.

In a sense, the art of acting is the art of contrived spontaneity, but there is a related characteristic which has repercussions for the drama teacher. Although I as a father may have feigned spontaneity, at least it was an expression of my anger; I *was* feeling angry. Now for the actor there is a critical difference: he is not angry; he is not *expressing* anger; he is portraying the character's expression of anger. The character's actions, not the actor's, imply some emotional disturbance in relation to some object in the character's fictitious world. It is Lear who is raging at the storm, not the actor. The *substance* of the actor's expression is his concern with effectiveness in representing Lear-raging-at-a-storm. But the *mode* of that expression is, like the second sigh, adjectival. The actor is seeing himself as an object of an audience's attention; he 'places' his presentation in their direction; his presentation is static rather than fluid; accessible to repetition, descriptive rather than experiential and, we can now add, in Tormey's (1971) terms the actor's behaviour is *not expressive* because the substance of what is being communicated to the audience is not expressive of the actor's ongoing emotional state. Tormey does not intend this conclusion should diminish the actor's achievement, rather the reverse, for as we shall see he wishes to make the point that all art is detached from expressive behaviour in the way it has been defined. This is not its weakness but its strength. For one of the features of expression is that some aspects of the subjective experience remain hidden from the observer. There is always a subjective aspect of my experiencing which I cannot communicate when I feel angry or sad or satisfied about something. In art, Tormey argues, there is nothing hidden; there is no inner consciousness that is not available to the observer. It is all there – on the canvas, in the musical rendering, on the stage – provided the observer is sensitive enough to respond to it. A play expresses, not the actor's or the playwright's emotional state. It expresses itself. Furthermore, what one character expresses is but one property of a complex whole. As Tormey puts it:

> We may, given the circumstances of the action of the drama, be justifiably certain that the cries of the protagonist are an expression of remorse, but this leaves unanswered the question of the expressive properties of the *play*. The drama itself may project pity, horror or contempt towards the remorse of the protagonist. (p139)

Thus what a play is about may be different from and even contradict a character's expressive behaviour.

On the basis of this theory as I have so far presented it, actor-training is concerned with developing skill in representation, a process of describing a character's emotional state. A director's responsibility lies beyond that to the overall meaning of the thing created, the play itself. The play must effectively express its own meaning.

Now what are the implications here for educationalists? Given that Malcolm Ross holds that drama is a performing art so that what is created must ultimately be shared with an audience, '... where interaction between maker and audience is part of the expressive process the audience being integral to the medium' (1982), one can perhaps understand how this allows him to see dramatic action as detached from emotion, for according to this model acting is a matter of demonstrating feeling not suffering it. When he talks of a 'cool' approach, emotion becomes some past reference point, projected through the medium of the character's gestures and words. When he talks of concentrating on the medium itself he means the technical craft of depictment and the director's overview of what is being communicated.

He closes his postscript with what really amounts to his credo:

> Above all we staked our work on the inherent, inexhaustible and sufficient interest of the dramatic problem. (p152)

And all this makes sense – provided one chooses to confine dramatic educational experience to this narrow view. I have made the point that in the postscript he does not really answer the central thrust of my chapter. The answer is he cannot. His view of drama is exclusive – there is no place for my conception of the subject.

For him, as for Tormey, an art product is about itself. And education in the arts, while putting one in touch with one's feelings, is not concerned with direct expression of them. Nor can it be concerned with learning about subject-matter. Such a pursuit is irrelevant if we are to let the art product 'speak for itself'. I find this persuasive. In using drama to get children to look at issues we may well be deflecting the child's attention from the arts process and indeed be failing him in his aesthetic education.

Arnaud Reid (1982) attempts to define aesthetic attitude:

> What is called the 'aesthetic' attitude or interest in an object, is sometimes described as a 'disinterested interest'. This is intended to mean that the object is attended to, and in some sense 'enjoyed for itself', 'for its own sake', for the qualities it possesses in itself as apprehended, and arouses our attention and interest. It is called 'disinterested' not, of course, because we are uninterested, but because it excludes extraneous or irrelevant interests, such as the interest in increasing our factual knowledge, or improving us morally, or in making a good investment by buying a picture. Aesthetic interest might, incidentally, achieve some or all of these other things: but aesthetically speaking they are irrelevant.

This appears to put most of what we do in drama in schools in a most unfortunate light. After this no one is going to rally to John Fines's banner! If you have been using drama to teach Road Safety to your infants, or what it is like to carry the burden of responsibility to your juniors or corruption in society today to your CSE drama group you'd better write yourselves off as artistic failures and take up plumbing!

But hold on a minute. Let us at least look at what does go on in the way many of us teach drama – we may find we are not as far astray as it appears. Let us begin by examining our practice, noting in particular those aspects which differ markedly from Malcolm Ross's views. First of all let us take self-expression in Tormey's sense of the word. We do encourage children during drama actually to feel sad about something in the fiction, or to be pleased or curious or disappointed or magnanimous or frustrated or amused or even angry.

129

These are not the raw emotions that worry Ross, for dramatic activity by definition is reflexive – any emotional disturbance is projected through the 'as-if' and raw emotion is tempered. But it is also a subjective experience with some facet of the disturbance remaining hidden. It is the emotional engagement with something outside oneself, filtered through the make-believe that has such a powerful learning potential. For instance, the child who in the drama experiences, perhaps for the first time, the pain, the effort and the joy of standing up for himself and not giving in to his peers, and who finds that because he is labelled John Smith, Explorer and the others in the class fellow adventurers, has personal resources he did not know were there for John Smith, *schoolboy*, must go through that pain and triumph over peer pressure. Other aspects of the curriculum (literature, for example) might 'tell' him about those feelings, but in drama he 'engages' with them – in a way he cannot do in real life. Nor would he reach the same change in understanding if he were required in drama to 'depict', for depiction or description tends to convey what is already understood rather than open up new meanings. There is, however, a built in protection in the 'as-if', protection from the exigencies and immediate confrontations of the actual present. The effect is not necessarily to reduce or water down the emotion, but to liberate it, so that John Smith may allow himself an emotional struggle he would not be prepared to cope with in the rawness of everyday living. Thus emotion in drama may be deeper, more intense than in 'real life', because it is safer.

Acting behaviour in this kind of work is experiential: it is the verb, not the adjective. In this it differs fundamentally from what the performer is doing. However, we need to modify our position here, for the way I have argued so far has suggested that the verb and adjective of expressive behaviour are mutually exclusive. This is not absolutely correct as we know, for instance, that certain actions can function as both without their external features changing – the sigh, for instance, was an example of this – but more importantly many instances of acting sustain a dialectic between the verb and the adjective.

I would like to put the point that performance for an audience *requires* description, while accepting that to varying degrees, varying in intensity, varying from actor to actor, from performance to performance, from style of play, from style of production, *etc, etc*, the actor may be expressing actual feelings. I would also like to claim that in drama work with children, whereas the nature of the work *requires* real feelings, it may also to varying degrees be descriptive. (Indeed because drama is social, a certain amount of describing must be going on – to *each other*.) That the expression of emotion is often qualified by this kind of dialectic is yet a further move away from the raw emotion of reactive behaviour.

Indeed many drama teachers have realised that where a topic is too 'near the bone' for a particular class – say, 'facing death' or 'street violence' or 'experiencing failure' – 'depiction' rather than a spontaneous improvisation may be both safer and more thoughtful.

One of the techniques used by drama teachers in recent years has been 'teacher-in-role', which Malcolm Ross (1978) sees as dangerously manipulative – like a teacher putting a stroke onto a child's painting. I can understand him seeing it that way, as that is what it sometimes looks like. But I want to suggest that 'teacher-in-role' is no more manipulative than showing the children a painting or stimulating them with a story or inspiring them with music, for 'teacher-in-role' is equivalent to what Ross calls 'realised form'. Teacher is never in the experience – she is always in the descriptive mode which automatically puts the pupils in a *spectator* relationship to her contribution (see Fleming, 1982). This provides yet another qualifying factor to the rawness of emotion. What the teacher does in her role is often very exciting for the children, but it is the excitement of a collective audience and collectively they can harness that excitement for their own actions, just as they would if teacher had read an exciting story.

And yet, of course, the purpose of 'teacher-in-role' is also to heighten the engagement of the children and direct interaction that is too heavily handled by the teacher, can spill over the boundaries of fiction. But these occurrences are relatively rare. (I can recall two occasions – one some years ago when I with too much suddenness frightened a class of four year olds, and more recently with a group of Cleveland head-teachers, I misjudged the distress level caused by a particularly strong use of teacher-in-role.)

To summarise, I have suggested that in children's drama a number of distancing processes are going on that protect children from reactive behaviours. One is that make-believe is essentially reflexive – I can channel my feelings *through* the role I am playing. The second is that it is never entirely experiential – there is in all dramatic playing at least an element of 'describing' or 'showing'. And thirdly, when 'teacher-in-role' is adopted, she is always 'describing', never experiencing with the children.

This may be fine as far as it goes, but I have avoided the apparently unanswerable challenge that we are depriving children of the aesthetic because so much concentration is on understanding not aesthetic form, but a drama's subject-matter. We busy ourselves with learning areas, objectives, concepts, generalisations and all the paraphernalia of educational respectability. Teachers of the other arts eschew such practice, for they know they are concerned with something different. Why is drama out of step?

I want now to suggest that we only appear to be out of step, for the whole practice of drama in schools is based on an assumption, using Arnaud Reid's definition of the term. It is an assumption made by the children, not the teacher. *The children's assumption is that the activity is 'for itself'.* Indeed if this were not the case no drama would ever get started, for it is this pleasure in making believe for its own sake that provides the critical motivation for doing it. Take it away and nothing can happen. This applies as much to the executive trainee, subjected to role-play simulation as to infants playing at witches. The executive must enjoy it for itself as he does other 'play' experiences such as cards, golf or fast cars. Teachers nowadays rarely talk about drama in this way, but even if they do not acknowledge the 'play' element in their drama work, they must at least subconsciously be catering for it. John Fines prizes this. He knows that drama has to have the fun of playing a game. When he was recently broached by a worried headmaster about how much history he thought a class of children had learnt, the answer he wanted to give was something like: 'Can you not see that these children within their drama were more animated in their conversation with each other than ever before? Who cares about history?' John is more than content with the joy of the playing.

But the drama 'game' can be a very sophisticated one, as children who work with John Fines and Ray Verrier discover. It is often set in quite an elaborate historical context requiring intellectual discipline and style in communication. He has no interest in keeping the game of drama at 'Snap' when they can cope with 'Monopoly'. The game's the thing and, *incidentally,* they will learn a great deal about Monopoly!

However determined the teacher may be to enrich the drama, he must always respect – indeed he has no choice but to respect – that the game is theirs and the practice of it *is satisfying in itself.* To re-quote Arnaud Reid, 'This is to mean that the object is attended to and in some sense 'enjoyed' for itself, 'for its own sake' ... (p4). Thus the play impulse, as Schiller (1965) has urged is the very basis of aesthetic experience and art and this same basis is the *sine qua non* of drama.

Now when children play they do not usually 'perform' their playing. Whether they are in role as a goal-keeper, a cowboy or a 17th-century Puritan, they express themselves experientially. They do not describe or demonstrate these roles; they experience the passion of them. There is, as Vygotsky (1976) has pointed out, a 'dual affect': ... the child weeps in play as a patient, but revels as a player' (p549). It is the revelling which sustains the notion of dramatic play for its own sake and because of this once more tempers the rawness of that passion in that process. It is this passion that the drama teacher can harness for educational ends. Drama, like literature, stands apart from the other arts in the sense that it draws directly on the world for its substance. The careful organisation of that material by the teacher makes the 'game' more elaborate and challenging. During the process of enjoying the drama the child's view of the world may be changed, but this can only happen because the child's need for satisfaction in doing drama was met.

Where the teacher doing the structuring has a strong sense of theatrical form, the playing can become something more than sophisticated interaction. Through careful selection of focus, tension and symbol (Bolton, 1979), the dramatic playing may be such that the playing experience becomes elevated to high drama, not achieved technically through participants' performances, but because their collective expressive behaviour is wrought by theatrical form. Drama is more than a performing art, dependent upon a final inter-action with an audience. Drama can be a group celebration to which there are no witnesses.

John Fines is right to promote the 'play-way' to education, but if he denies the value of drama as a subject in its own right, then I think he is wrong to do so. Malcolm Ross is right to recognise the importance of drama as a performing art, but he is wrong to see it as exclusively this. I invite them both, occasionally, to join me in the middle of the field, where children can learn about them-selves and the world around them through the potency of a dramatic moment.

Education and dramatic art:
a personal review

In *Education and dramatic art*, the first edition of which came out in 1989, David Hornbrook delivered a swingeing attack on drama in education and on Heathcote and Bolton in particular (see Introduction). Bolton wrote his own personal review of the book, which appeared in the National Association of Drama's *Drama Broadsheet* (the forerunner to their *Journal for Drama in Education*) in the Spring edition, 1990.

Education and Dramatic Art by David Hornbrook
Blackwell Education, 1989

This book is the story of a builder who was so anxious that people should believe his new house to be different from anyone else's that he demolished all the other houses first, so that all that was good about the old houses would be forgotten.

In spite of a disclaimer in the Preface, the reader of this book is led to expect to learn about a new approach to drama education. The author, David Hornbrook, expends a great deal of energy, through many pages, arguing how nearly everyone so far has failed to grasp the fundamental purpose of drama in schools and that he, David Hornbrook, has the answers. We are to understand that drama teachers (with the exception of a few Comprehensive School Heads of Department) do not know what they are doing and that the authors in the field have spent their professional years misleading others. One can hardly wait to learn what the alternative is to be, but when one reads towards the end of the book, 'The formulation of dramatic art, therefore, represents not a new set of rules and methodologies but rather a conflation of the best of existing practice in the field of drama education', one doesn't know whether to be relieved that one might have been doing the right things after all or to be astonished that he has spent so many pages expressing hostility to other people's work to so little purpose. Neither of these reactions would be appropriate, for if one puts on one side Hornbrook's obvious antagonism towards his drama colleagues, one can discover that some of his arguments are indeed worthy of consideration. As a greater part of his hostility is aimed at me, it makes it difficult for me to use the kind of detachment one would normally expect of a reviewer. I have sought the editor's permission to write a personal response to the book. At the same time I hope I shall give a fair account.

For David Hornbrook there is a 'vacuum at the centre of drama-in-education theory' (p6). The whole book puts forward a coherent explanation of this view and he attempts to fill that vacuum with a cultural/political model drawn from the Marxist-flavoured thinking of writers such as Raymond Williams, Clifford Geertz, Alisdair MacIntyre and Charles Taylor. His attack on drama education theorists is based on what he sees as a fundamental misconception, which has resulted in a distorted view of dramatic art and superficial, rudderless practice. It is difficult to disentangle the strands of his argument without appearing to over-simplify, but for the sake of this review, I propose to look at his thesis under the three headings of: (1) individualism (2) learning and (3) dramatic art.

Individualism

Like other writers before him, Hornbrook chooses to demonstrate how the Rousseauesque cultivation of the individual in society has led to an over-emphasis by 'progressive' educationalists on the importance of the individual in society and in the classroom, this philosophy in turn affected the way drama teachers saw their subject. I myself have made this point on a number of occasions and in 1984 I wrote as follows:

> And I wish to argue further that in using drama to promote the individual's growth we have inadvertently distorted drama itself on two counts. The first is that drama is never about oneself; it is always concerned with something outside oneself. And secondly, drama is a social event and not a solitary experience. ... Yet we have trained a generation of teachers who think that drama is just this, that it is an expression of each child's ego, so that a bewildered teacher feels a responsibility not towards what is being created by a group of thirty, but towards thirty individual creations. Drama is not about self-expression... (*Drama as Education* by Gavin Bolton, Longman, 1984)

I can recall with horror trying to work with groups of students in the early '70s who had been trained to believe that each individual's self-centred creativity was paramount – and I as teacher was expected to nurture the delicate blossoming. To my astonishment, in his historical survey, Hornbrook places my work firmly within this 'individualist' school of thought! He dismissively refers to 'Bolton's individualism'. We shall see that for some reason Hornbrook chooses to put my writings and my work in the worst possible light. He must think that this somehow strengthens his argument. On the whole however this is a very interesting historical survey, including aspects of political strands and recent developments that give a fuller picture than has so far been published.

Learning

Here again I am the target for his criticism. I once wrote that we must not expect all drama to be **art**, that providing some kind of learning is going on, the teacher should not feel too frustrated. Now the idea of drama having any function other than an artistic one is anathema to David Hornbook. Presumably he sees no place in school for using dramatic method to teach, for example, Road Safety to infants. This kind of pedagogy, he maintains, has undermined Drama as a subject and should not be tolerated. He uses the term 'drama pedagogy' more and more disparagingly as he proceeds with his argument, so that we are taken by surprise when towards the end of the book he admits that effective art must '...challenge us with the revelation of the new' (p106), and later he suggests that drama is about 'making sense of ourselves' and by page 110 he confesses that 'Drama is a 'learning medium' to the extent that all art is' (thus still excluding my Road Safety example but at least he is using the term 'learning medium'). He adds that, 'We may regard dramatic art not so much as another way of knowing, but rather as a way of participating in dramatic conversations which can lead to new perceptions, to **us making better sense of things**' (my emphasis).

For David Hornbrook, the resistance to phrases like 'a way of knowing' is part of a more general disapproval of what he calls the 'psychologising' of drama. One of his reasons for his criticism of me is that I have spent much of my professional career in drawing up theories related to what goes on in the head when we participate in drama. I can see that from Hornbrook's point of view such theorising takes teachers into an educational *cul-de-sac* especially when it comes to fighting for drama as a subject in the present political climate. Unfortunately his opposition takes the form of taking extreme positions. He finds it unacceptable, for example, that I claim that drama requires a special 'mental state' (p61). This seems to me to be so self-evident (a child bestriding a narrow stream has the choice of deciding whether or not there are croco-diles in the water – the action involved may not change, but what is going on in the head is different) one wonders why Hornbrook allows himself to be side-tracked from the main thrust of his argument.

He is right to draw our attention to epistemological confusion in drama in education theory, including my own. For years now I have tried to adopt a position that, while denying the subjectivity of child-centred drama, nevertheless clings to the notion of 'Personal knowing' in dialectical relationship to 'Objective knowing'. Now Hornbrook is seeking a model which transcends the subjective/objective opposition. His reading of Michael Polanyi, who poses the critical factor of intellectual responsibility in the shaping of knowledge, takes Hornbrook some way towards breaking away from the subjective/ objective trap but, as we shall see, only the Marxist view of culturally determined knowledge will satisfy him.

He takes issue with me over such phrases of mine as 'The learning ... has to be felt for it to be effective' (p78). For him this is just another confirmation that I belong to the 'individualist' school. This is to misunderstand that many of us were trying to find different ways of breaking away from the feeling and thinking dualism of traditional education. Raymond Williams, Hornbrook's own guru, expresses the importance of feeling-in-thinking with, '..not feelings against thought, but thought as felt and feeling as thought...' (p103). Thus this kind of thinking/feeling metaphor is okay – providing his drama colleagues don't use it!

Hornbrook is also obsessively condemnatory of 'universals'. Confusion there may be at a theoretical level (I have tended to refer to levels of generality; others have intended more mystical meanings) but my impression is that the debate remains academic for most teachers and does not warrant the considerable attention Hornbrook seems to think necessary. He does usefully draw attention, however, to the vexed question of the relationship between the particularity of a dramatic event and the generalities to be drawn from it. Now I am berated by Hornbrook for over-emphasising the thematic at the expense of the particularity of the event. I cannot accept this, for the moment one uses drama one is **in** a particularity. This is what is exciting about drama in that it is the most concrete of art forms. But there must be some resonance from the particular to other levels of apprehension. When Shylock brandishes his knife Shakespeare is conveying rather more than idiosyncratic behaviour of a particular Shylock in a particular city of Venice on a particular date. Bruner has done some research on children's ability to 'read' at more than one level of meaning – and any work on attainment targets in drama must include assessment of this ability.

But Hornbrook makes an additional point in this connection: that drama in the classroom provides teachers with an opportunity to deal directly with political issues. He complains that I tend to avoid such a head-on approach (and he is right – I believe it to be a matter of a teacher's personal choice; I neither encourage nor check my own student-teachers) but for Hornbrook this verges on criminality. He writes, 'Drama then becomes a form of reduction to the obvious, its learning objectives triumphantly achieved only because they are so undemanding' (p81). After taking this blow between the eyes it is more than a little surprising to find that he is also critical of those radical practitioners such as Warwick Dobson, who do indeed advocate the direct approach he would have me follow (p85).

Dramatic Art

David Hornbrook still prefers to pursue the myth that his colleagues in drama are anti-theatre. For instance he believes that we *see* drama in terms of **process** only. This is nonsense. I among others have for many years been talking about 'making a drama' of 'making a play' etc. where clearly a **product** is implied. I have always stressed that that must be the focus for the participants. In the lengthy quote from my book above, I use the phrase 'what is being created', an implied object that can be reflected upon. (Hornbrook himself uses the terms 'critical appraisal or reflection'). He also uses a terminology I myself have been employing in recent years when I have invited my classes to '**read**' the '**text**' of what has been created.

But on my attempts to identify theatrical elements in **all** drama he pours scorn. I believe that just as there are recognisable basic elements to games, so there exist essential elements of art including drama. I am talking about the deliberate manipulation, for example, of time, space, sound and colour which I have observed in the play of pre-school children and which somehow gets lost as a result of traditional education. I have called it dramatic **form**. Unfortunately, Hornbrook and I are at cross-purposes because when he uses the word 'form', he really means 'genre' (p106 and other places). His scorn of my interpretation of form rests on a deep opposition to the possibility of non-performance drama. He writes, 'It is my contention that conceptually there is *nothing* (my italics) which differentiates the child acting from the actor on the stage in the theatre' (p104). Now this is where Hornbrook and I differ fundamentally, fundamentally because this standpoint seriously affects the structuring of the drama, pupil/teacher expectations of the outcome and subsequent reflection and evaluation. At a philosophical level one could agree with Hornbrook's argument that dramatic activity is always a performance because even the child in solitary play is an audience to him/herself – just as in 'real life' one is an observer of one's solitary actions. The conclusion would have to be therefore that all activity is of the same kind, a bizarre conclusion which, however logically sound in terms of audience awareness, is not in the least bit useful to anyone. We all know from real life how different it feels if, say, one is about to reprimand one's off-spring only to discover that a stranger is watching you! In **practice** the degree to which one is aware of an audience matters a great deal And the same applies to drama. A group of junior school children absorbed as 'rescuers' working out how to get their friend out of the sheriff's dungeon are operating in the dramatic 'present' and the notion of 'performing' it has little relevance. They are 'making' drama with no concern beyond finding a solution to a problem. Performance, on the other hand, is to do with communicability to non-participants, with repeatability and with characterisation and as such requires a different set of skills – and a different form of evaluation. I would expect such a performance mode (including performance at its simplest level in, for instance, 'tableau' presentations) to be employed for 90 per cent of the time in upper-Secondary School drama and virtually none (5%?) of the time in the kindergarten class. For all his insistence that there is no difference, Hornbrook finds himself writing, 'reproduction ... describes ... any activity where the children are concentrating on the **performance** rather than the **making** of a text' (p105). I believe 'making' and 'performing', while both part of dramatic art, are in certain respects critically different – requiring a different mental set, perhaps!

Now in his Preface Hornbrook takes pleasure in reporting that at a recent conference 90 per cent of the arts delegates 'voted for attainment targets...' (pxi). This is obviously something close to Hornbrook's heart. But if, as his book demonstrates, he cannot see any difference between children doing drama for themselves and children performing on stage, if he cannot recognise that concrete dramatic action on stage and in the classroom is open to many levels of meaning, if he refuses to acknowledge that dramatic art has an inner form to do with, for example, tension created by the manipulation of space, how can he possibly be ready to consider assessment in dramatic art? It may well be that because of his influential position he is at present advising government bodies and others on attainment targets.

David Hornbrook's Model

I may have given the impression that David Hornbrook is simply using the book to take swipes in arbitrary directions. This is far from the case for all his criticism (sound or otherwise) stems from a firm rationale. His thesis is that most drama in education theory relies too heavily on Platonic or Freudian or Phenomenological views of, respectively, the rational or inner or personal being, and that our attempts to resolve the conflicting claims of rationalism and empiricism and of subjectivity and objectivity are misplaced. What all these models of humans and of humans' attempts to 'know' fail to grasp is that all thought **and all feelings** are culturally determined. Hornbrook argues persuasively that, for example, my continual use of such phrases as 'sensing the rightness of something' or 'feeling in their bones' is without sense unless I go beyond them to look at the culture that has given meaning to those feelings: as Hornbrook puts it, '**...we learn to know what to feel**' (p102).

Only by disengagement from the psychological burden of thoughts and feelings can we bring coherence to the task of making judgements about both content and form in respect of the making of or the performing of a 'text'. The teacher's task, at first as 'a guide and collaborator in the interpretative project' (p122), becomes that of a **critic** who 'takes the 'adequate' comprehensions of the group, and subjects them to analysis, questioning the motivations and interests which are implicit in those comprehensions, exposing their origin, their distortions, and the purposes and functions they serve' (p123). The points of reference are not inwards but outwards towards a hermeneutic circle of modification in which judgements are made and remade about the drama created. This critical standpoint submits the drama to *ideologiekritik*, an examination of the power behind the language and actions.

But more than this, David Hornbrook wants to bring a moral imperative to the judgment. One of the dangers for young people endlessly role-playing in drama is that, as with much sociological theorising about social roles, the only criterion of achievement is one of 'effectiveness' and that 'moral choices' are seen as dispensable. For Hornbrook the difference between social role and **character** lies in the moral dimension which the latter brings. I found this very interesting and would have liked examples of its application.

Implications of Hornbrook's Models for the Classroom

Sorry, he must be keeping them a secret. This is the biggest let down. The reader is left thirsting for examples of practice showing how the teacher as guide, interpreter and critic operates in a drama lesson, how the application of his model gives a new and refreshing look to work with infants, juniors and secondary pupils. He refers to one Secondary example to do with 'exploring relationships within the family', but he does not give us the text of the lesson; he merely assures us that such a lesson (where they get into groups and make up a scene ready to show! – staggeringly innovative!) is amenable to the application of his model. It is we who are left with a vacuum indeed.

Final Comment

In his first chapter Hornbrook writes with some assumed amazement that 'Even after her retirement from Newcastle in 1986, past accounts of Heathcote's drama workshops were still being dissected and analysed by her admirers for the wisdoms they might offer up' (p15). I wonder whether he realises now that this kind of comment tells us a great deal about David Hornbrook.

David, when your and my names are long forgotten, teachers will still be learning from Dorothy Heathcote.

Piss on his face

This is Bolton's keynote address delivered to the National Association of Teachers of Drama/National Drama Joint National Conference at Didsbury, Easter, 1992. It is a humourous, self-deprecating, but pungent riposte to David Hornbrook's attacks on DiE.

My research shows that there aren't too many conference addresses with this particular title. According to your sensibilities its crudeness may either make you want to hear more or close your ears to the rest. If I tell you that it is an actual quote, this may make it less offensive. If I go on to tell you that is is a quote from an eight year old boy in the most disastrous teaching experience of my career, you may feel you have a professional interest and be ready to offer me some sympathy, especially those of you who teach that age group.

It happened last October. I am not going to go into all the embarrassing details of a total lesson failure, but I am going to describe the beginnings of the lesson up to the point of the above line of dialogue. Part of the trouble was that I was positively oozing with arrogance when I entered the classroom to find these sweet-faced innocents sitting in a huddle on the story-corner carpet. Earlier that day I had managed some success with the 11 year olds in the same school and over lunch the staff who had been observing told me I could work magic. And I believed them!

The class-teacher of the afternoon class had warned me that one child in the class was 'highly disturbed', but we agreed she should not tell me which child that was. A few seconds into the lesson, I thought I had identified the one, but then quickly changed my mind because there was another one ... and another ... and another ...

I asked them what they would like to do some drama about, a ploy I typically use when I do not know the children. We put a list of possible subjects on the blackboard and they voted for ghosts. I wished afterwards that I'd used a postal vote! ... signs of intimidation were emerging. Reading warning signals I began cautiously: I pretended to creep to a door as though hearing an alarming noise from the other side, ... and asked them what they observed ... so far so good ... I then opened the door and said I couldn't see anything ... so we got onto 'invisibility'. Now this is where I should have tested the ground a step at a time by first bringing out one child to demonstrate how I 'couldn't see' him or her. But over-confident Bolton jumps a few steps and literally goes in with both feet. I asked them all to be invisible, sitting just where they were but shuffling into a slightly bigger carpet area so that I could move between them. The 'shuffling' seemed to take hours ... some squabbling ... some fighting ... and a few comforting phrases such as 'I don't want to do this' thrown in. Eventually quietened down I started to put on my act of creeping among invisible beings. I should have stopped altogether at this point ... that one or two of them put their arms around my knees trying to pull me to the ground, should have been sufficient warning that I was in an environment unfriendly! If only I had heeded that warning ... If only I had drawn a close on the drama, taken Peter Abbs's advice and told them about their cultural heritage!

But the cameras continued to whirr, so I persisted, still believing I had enough strategies up my sleeve to 'win them over'. After doing one or two more activities altogether during which a number of boys started to hide under desks, I decided to use a different space – a **working** area – their classroom desks. So, with them all back in their own desks facing the front, I felt I was back in control. I explained how I was going to pick *one* of them to come to the front of the class to be our 'invisible' ghost. From a lot of hands going up it was unfortunate that I picked the one child I thought had sufficient commitment and maturity to set a standard of acting behaviour for us – I was right about his ability, but I did not appreciate that he was an eight year old intruder from another class who wasn't able to attend swimming that afternoon. Thus to my question, 'Now how shall we make our ghost visible' came the answer, 'Piss on his face!'

All my theoretical understanding of drama flashed through my mind. Clearly this was drama: 'a ghoul in a mess'! Was there some universal I should 'drop to'? Or had we already 'dropped'? Where did 'constraint' come in? And what about tension and symbolisation – those faithful band-aids of drama teaching, both lurking there somewhere. Where were those 'bones' I'm always saying I know things in? They all failed me and I did what teachers do the world over – I used the 'get-out' clause. With a grim, Joyce Grenfell kind of smile on my face I said brightly: 'Does anyone else have an idea?'

I won't bore you with further details just yet – it got worse. In fact I would prefer you to keep this professional failure to yourself – within these four walls. I wouldn't want the Arts Council Drama Education Working Group to hear about it. They'll tell me I should have turned it into a performance for school assembly!

I may have failed to find a theatrical metaphor that caught those children's interest, but I propose to use the title of this address as a metaphor now – a metaphor for **ways of effecting change**.

It is one thing to see the need for change in drama education; it is another matter to know how to effect that change. One way is to make a personal attack on someone; to 'Piss on his face'; it's sometimes called the Hornbrook approach. I know what it is like to be at the receiving end of David Hornbrook's excretory discharge. One thing I have discovered is that it is very difficult to hear what someone is saying when he is pissing on your face.

Now Hornbrook is advocating change. Why he should adopt his particularly insensitive method is more to do with ego building than with an honest ex-position of theory. Nevertheless he is right to be advocating change and once we've wiped the urine from our faces we should give attention to what he is saying. In fact what he is saying needs our closest attention for where he is talking sense he offers pointers worth following but where he is mistaken, he is plausible, naive, ignorant and dangerous.

His misconceptions are fundamental, but let us first look at areas where I agree with him.

I believe that for too long some teachers have ignored 'development in drama' as an important objective. About five years ago I sat in at an In-service Course for teachers. In an early session the tutor invited the teachers in small groups to 'brain storm' all the objectives they could think of related to their classroom practice. As you can imagine the lists were very long, going from 'Giving a sense of well-being' to 'learning about the subject-matter'. No group mentioned the possibility of their pupils getting better at Drama. When I commented on this to the class they looked at me as though I had committed some heresy. Now this seems to be to be seriously negligent. Hornbrook has rightly drawn attention to this gap.

I believe that we have given too much attention to drama as a process, *at the expense of* seeing it as a product. It seems to me that when we invite children to 'make' drama – I think the term 'making' is useful – we and they know they are making *something*. I like David Hornbrook's use of the term 'text' to cover

145

a wide conception of the 'something' that is made. However, whereas I believe process and product *both* need our attention, especially when it comes to evaluating, I am worried that Hornbrook appears to discount the former.

I believe that Hornbrook is right that we and our pupils together should evaluate the drama work. I have been remiss in not tackling this issue and I am still not in a position to recommend a detailed frame within which to operate. The result of this neglect is that Alistair Black, under the auspices of the Arts Council, has produced a document, a large section of which is devoted to an evaluation system based on a concept of drama which is largely audience orientated. There is a disconcerting unevenness in the attainment targets, which denigrate experiential dramatic playing by its omission. Even improvisation is always seen as something done for an audience.

I believe Hornbrook is right that a mystique has developed round the teaching of drama that invites teachers to feel they are failures.

I believe David Hornbrook is right when he complains that not enough attention has been given to helping those teachers who are involved in examination Drama. The *study* by adolescents of Drama as an arts subject has not been part of major publications on Drama education. The whole focus from writers like Dorothy Heathcote and myself and others has been on processes of dramatic engagement rather than the study and performance of texts. This is something that needs rectifying – by adjusting the balance **not** by replacement.

In these matters it is my view that David Hornbrook should be listened to; more attention needs to be given: to development in our pupils' ability to handle drama, to the recognition of a 'drama product', to the need for a framework for evaluation (he has produced a crude, audience oriented, impractical model) but he is right to recognise the *need* for evaluation, to the need for a clearer way of talking about methods, and to the lack of attention to the study of drama at the upper end of the Secondary School. There are fundamental issues however about which he should be challenged.

My guess is that Hornbrook has been deprived as a teacher and as a participant of the richness that experiential drama can provide. Because he does not understand it, Hornbrook would prefer that others did away with it. He has missed out on the sheer joy it can bring to all kinds of children, from the linguistically under-achieving to the most able, from the emotionally unstable to the most mature, from the least to the most talented.

I believe that experiential play-making (i.e. drama without an audience) provides the basis for the best drama training that a more formal Upper Secondary Theatre course could build upon – Hornbrook does not want to know.

I believe it teaches the principal elements of theatre, a feature of the work which Hornbrook does not want to acknowledge.

I believe that the use of 'teacher-in-role' as an approach to drama is the most important strategy in the teacher's repertoire. I am pleased to see it does at least creep into the Arts Council Publication in two of the examples, but, alas, it is not given any place in that document's theoretical comments.

I believe that Hornbrook's 'Christopher Columbus' example is laughable in its naiveté. It is certainly proper for the occasional presentation of work in assembly to be seen as one minor expression of drama work for Primary School pupils, but does he not realise that the pupils who would be most effective in trying out his particular example are likely to be those who have had a grounding in the kind of drama he purports to despise.

I believe all theorising in drama should be drawn from *practice*. Hornbrook's practice is empty of substantially new ideas; he does not have anything new to offer apart from widening the scope of theatre art and craft for examination students. He has then made this his base-line, from which he works backwards down to Key Stage 1 – and, I'm sorry to say, Alistair Black and his panel have swallowed it in relation to Attainment targets. All the examples for 7 and 11 year olds have audience orientated overtones, and yet from the introductory exposition one is led to expect that attainment might also relate to Drama for Understanding. I too want young children to develop skills in theatre, but I believe there are good reasons for delaying teaching children formal performance 'tricks' at too early an age. Indeed some Theatre Schools complain that they have to 'undo' bad habits acquired in School Productions.

Hornbrook in his first book expressed amazement that he came across some teachers who were still analysing video tapes of Heathcote's work. I believe Dorothy Heathcote is a genius whose work will be studied and better understood generations from now. She is out of the reach of most of us. I would love to invite her and David Hornbrook each to take the topic of Columbus' discovery of America with a class of 11 year olds!

Our profession is going through a bad time. It does not help matters that Hornbrook thinks he is offering something that has to be seen as an *alternative*. What we need is a new *emphasis*, building on the strengths of the past, learning from its weaknesses, not a pendulum swinging in one or other direction. Pissing on people's faces may give a lot of satisfaction if you have the temperament for it, but is has caused a lot of damage at a time when we need to be as strong as possible. The profession generally has already been pissed on by a Mr. Kenneth Clarke, and is no doubt steeling itself for an assault from John Patten[1]. We don't have to do it to each other. It is time for *dialogue*, for *listening*. More important than carrying the same membership label, important as that may be, is that we are willing to learn from each other where there are differences ... and build on each other's strengths ... and perhaps laugh a little more together.

I propose now to conclude with a brief description of what happened next in my 'ghost' lesson. The class agreed after some time that the way to make the ghost visible was to use a knife on him, which action apparently (this was straight from a current television programme) would cause slime to ooze out until he could be fully exposed. So, I picked a girl to be the one to take the 'knife'. I asked her to stand at the rear of the class with the blade held high; I did some awesome narration (in suitably modulated tones!) inviting her to approach the victim slowly. As she started off, looking like Medea at her most murderous, a boy suddenly jumped up from his seat and, with a pretend knife in his hand, rushed to the still figure of the ghost and drew a circle round the area of his genitals, 'cut them out' and 'flung them' on the floor! A ghoul without goolies drama!

Thanks, David Hornbrook, I prefer to be pissed on!

And my research shows that there aren't too many conferences addresses that end with that particular line.

Note
1 Both Conservative Education Ministers in the 1980s.

Have a Heart!

First published in *Drama* (the Journal of National Drama) in Vol 1, Summer 1992. It is unusual in form and style as it is, unlike his usual measured articles, perhaps Bolton's most sarcastic and hard-hitting piece of writing, written in response to Peter Abbs's accusations of Bolton's form of drama destroying our cultural heritage. All emphases as in original.

Now I understand what the problem is: you have painted yourself into a corner. Reading between the lines of your text I now realise you are outside the creative activity you are criticising. You do not know what it is like to experience the theatrical excitement of a group created drama; you do not 'know' what it is like to be with children who are prepared to bring their whole selves and not just their techniques to their art; you do not 'know' it from the inside either as an artist/teacher or as an artist/participant. Such an experience has never been important to you and you cannot be expected to understand its spiritual, intellectual and aesthetic power. Your concept of classroom drama is something 'functional' you have read about in books. Your heart is not touched by the love of drama nurtured in our pupils over the last twenty to thirty years.

From your distant corner you opportunistically have added support to the notion that whatever was going on in drama in schools needed to be displaced. What you seem to have discovered is something called 'culture' and to demonstrate your theatre erudition you give long lists of theatrical movements from the Greeks to Kathakali (missing out, dear me, Roman Theatre, Jacobean, Restoration, Comedie Francaise, Melodrama and Japanese Kabuki etc.). That you and I can reel off theatrical labels does not mean anything. You keep referring to Greek Theatre as though by labelling it you can make some claim to cultural endowment which others do not have. I happen to have directed part of the Theban trilogy, played the role of Creon and directed Anouilh's version of *Antigone* – how's that for a bit of cultural one-upmanship?

Working from the **inside** of theatre I know that what I do in the classroom is part of our cultural heritage. You seem to be prepared to accept 'Modern Theatre in all its variety' – but not if it includes classroom drama. To you what children are creating today, even if they care deeply about it, does not matter – with the exception of course of 'Columbus meeting natives' acted for Primary school assembly. Where does this laughable example fit into your grand cultural concept?

Of course you do not **want** to see theatre in my work. Your thesis is simple. Because what I do does not fit in with your narrow theory of aesthetics it cannot be considered as art. Cornered as you are, your one intent is to diminish and destroy. For instance you know I regard elements such as 'tension', 'contrast', 'ritual', 'constraint' and 'symbolisation' as fundamental to theatre experience. By you this becomes reduced to a patronising concession: '...in your own writing' you concede to me '...you have taken some of your concepts ... from the tradition of theatre and arts discourse ... it is true that your work has *not been devoid* (my italics) of 'the practices of theatre'.

There is something depressingly negative in your formulation – to coin a phrase. But notice also that you refer to my **writings**, not to the dramatic art I am engaged in, as though you cannot look at the practice of art, only its filtered form. Do you see art as something to be pondered on from the safety of your library-corner of 12 volumes on aesthetic education?

When I look at you in your corner, I can understand you want so badly to be seen offering a superior, alternative form of drama education; I am reminded of some drama work I have done several times over the last few years based on the text of an early folk-tale (sorry if this work with script mars your image of what 'educational drama' should be). It tells the story of a young man who is deceived into believing that he can only gain the heart of a young woman by cutting out the heart of his Mother.

I firmly believe that much of the work done in the drama classroom creates a rich soil from which actor-training or academic study of theatre can grow. (The last three decades of schooling have turned out some very good actors, don't you think?) It has never been within the scope of my professional work to train Drama Specialists for upper Secondary pupils. If it ever became my responsibility, I hope I would recommend that Drama be taught in a way that continued to give them faith in their own culture while opening up the riches of theatrical heritage, yes, from 'Sophocles to Caryl Churchill' (Are you excluding Aeschylus, by the way?: he came before Sophocles – just teasing!)

Do you really understand what you are condemning? You drop in jargon phrases like 'Mantle of the Expert' and 'Teacher-in-role'. There is no sense of your having been there, but you've learnt the words, so that gives you the right to persuade teachers to turn their back on one kind of practice in order to be part of your 'unstoppable' movement. And then, after arguing passionately, using such damning phrases as 'cut off from the aesthetic field'... 'forfeited any sense of intrinsic identity'... 'devoid of art'... 'devoid of the practices of theatre and critical terminology', you have the nerve to recommend in your last paragraph that 'the **dynamic approach** fostered by educational drama must be kept'!!!! Whatever for, if it is 'cut off from the aesthetic field' and 'devoid of art'? Are you now trying to have it both ways? I believe your criticism to be irresponsible. You have jumped on a pro-Hornbrook bandwagon, while building yourself an escape hatch!

That does not mean, of course, that criticism is out of place. Any professional movement in art or education is characterised by both its strengths and weaknesses, a strength in that new thinking about theory and practice emerges, a weakness in that we make mistakes, we try to deal with things only half-understood, we overemphasise, we neglect, we fail to re-focus when the time is ripe, we build theory out of theory instead of out of practice, or we see it as an opportunity for personal ambition. I am prepared to listen to and learn – and I have a lot to learn – from criticism, but it must come from someone who cares about what I am doing, not from someone who 'stands by' the view that my work is 'devoid of art', 'devoid of the practices of theatre' etc.

The relationship between Theatre and Education has always been a complex and enigmatic one – this is part of its excitement. You say 'The critique of (what you call) educational drama began some time ago' but then you only go as far back as 1979, referring to a publication by John Allen.

We can go back much further than that – for instance, a Ministry of Education report dated 1948, before you and I started teaching, discusses the issue remarkably fully and fairly. Pretty smart of those HMI to anticipate the Post Modernist impulse, don't you think?

I suggest you come out of your corner, come away from your shelf of 12 books and start to enjoy and delight in the complexity of the tension between theatre and education – in its **practice**. Help us find a way of travelling astride both paths. Let your heart engage with both. The kind of writing you and David Hornbrook indulge in makes it very difficult to hold a respectful dialogue. You invite other professionals to score points rather than share understanding. Is there **nothing**, absolutely **nothing**, that you could learn from us?

So he killed his mother ... And cut out her heart .... When he stumbled and fell, his Mother's heart said ... 'Are you hurt my son?'

Although

This was Gavin Bolton's Response to the National Curriculum Council Arts in Schools Project *The Arts 5-16*. It was a paper read to the NATD Conference 'The Next Step' on 20 October 1990 and appeared in *Drama Broadsheet*, Winter 1990,Vol.7 no.3

On pages 11 and 12 of *The Arts 5-16*, the writers give a brief background history of Drama Education which includes a reference to Dorothy Heathcote and me as elaborators of 'techniques of drama as a teaching method across the curriculum'. It continues: 'Although (when one hears an 'although', one braces oneself!) these techniques draw on forms and conventions of theatre, their emphasis has been on the use of drama as a method of exploring issues across the curriculum'. By this 'although' I feel nicely disposed of, relegated to a 'slot' in the history of drama education, a slot that will somehow turn out to be much inferior to what the writers have in mind. Could it be that they have fallen for the recent 'Bolton is anti drama as art' disinformation? Surely not. These are open minded people, trained in close observation of drama practice; they have only to see me working to realise that... Although, I could not help but notice, in their very next sentence, they do mention a David Hornbrook...

I am not really so egocentric that I can only respond to a newly published document in terms of my own work, although I am concerned that the very impulse that causes them to be dismissive of a particular approach as 'methodology' has also led them to offer a framework that, as far as drama is concerned, is basically flawed.

In attempting to define the arts, the writers make the following assertions with which I am in agreement:

> The arts ... are concerned with many different ways of knowing the world... (p26 A curriculum framework)

> The arts... are concerned not only with what we perceive in the world, but with the qualities of human perceptions; with how we experience the world. (*ibid*)

> They may also be creative in the more profound sense of generating new ways of seeing. (p27, *ibid*)

> ...at some times the artist is an iconoclast who challenges the prevailing attitudes and values; at other, artists are 'the voice of the community', shaping images and artefacts to give form to a community's deepest values and convictions. (*ibid*)

The above statements more or less represent my own credo. For the last thirty years this has been my understanding of what drama is about and I have spent those years professionally attempting to find ways of (to summarise the above statements) creating drama to help young people to know the world, to refine and challenge the ways in which they see the world, to examine how they relate to the world and to test their own society's values. Sometimes I have not done this very well – and I am still learning. All my writings have been to this end, to take teachers with me, to try to make these things happen in the classroom. Thus to the question 'What is the teaching and learning going on in your classroom today?', the first answer must most often be to do with some aspect referred to in the above quotations.

But if we read on in *Arts 5-16*, we astonishingly discover that the writers do not really see the arts in these terms at all. One might have reasonably expected that their statements above would provide the base-line of all their thinking about the arts curriculum, that their belief in their stated philosophy would provide the dynamic for the rest of the two volumes. No, this is not the case – and the reason for turning their back on their own stated philosophy also lies behind why they want to relegate mine and other people's work to 'methodology'. It becomes clear that in their view, if you should be so foolish as to take their initial claims for the arts literally, if you actually identify the aspect of life the children's drama is attempting to explore (which I have always tried to do), then you have undersold drama as art – and even if your pupils think they are making up a play and even if it seems they are working in theatre form, hard luck, you have gone down the slippery slope to methodology – and this is only useful in so far as it serves the buzz word of 'cross-discipline', and should be thought of as 'education-through-the-arts'. They may say drama is to do with getting to know the world, but if you actually practice on that assumption, even if the teacher and participants are consciously handling the elements of theatre, 'getting to know the world' gets relabelled as 'curriculum'.

They give some attention to 'issues across the curriculum', particularly in relation to the Primary school. In their second volume, *The Arts 5-16 Practice and Innovation*, one come across this kind of phrase in their chapter headed *The role of the arts in the Primary Curriculum*: 'The following accounts' – they are about to give sample lessons – 'illustrate the kinds of contribution the arts can make to the whole curriculum in *thematic, personal* and *social* and *artistic* terms.' (p38 – my emphasis). Now notice this separation of 'thematic' and 'artistic'. For the writers they are alternative ways of looking at the children's art work. They seek support for their argument from *English from 5-16* (DES, 1984), which does indeed have some positive suggestions about the outcome of regular practice in drama, but they are uncritical of this document for relegating drama to categories of 'listening and speaking' (No 'althoughs' for the DES).

So where do the hearts of the writers lie? It becomes overpoweringly clear that the reason for the whole project has been to promote what they call 'education-in-the-arts'. This, they claim, is something distinct from but complementary to 'education-through-the-arts'. Now it is in discussing elements of learning in terms of concepts, skills, attitudes and information that they are most at home – that is of course concepts about art, skills needed for art, attitudes towards art, and information about art. They try from time to time to redress the balance by such comments as: 'Secondary schools tend to emphasise learning in the arts and miss equally important opportunities to use the arts to enrich the curriculum as a whole.' (p7 *The Arts 5-16 Practice and Innovation*.) But I believe the arts are the curriculum, not something that sometimes serves the curriculum and sometimes is separate from it.

No doubt there is a relatively unimportant use of dramatic method occurring in schools which is adopted for the purpose of making the learning of facts or skills in other subject areas more palatable. Sometimes called Simulation, it has as much relationship to drama as drawing a diagram of something has to visual art. Both simulation role-play and diagrams have their place as part of a range of teaching techniques within other subject teachers' repertoires, but cannot be given serious consideration as part of a discussion about drama or visual art. I wonder if they think this is the kind of drama I do? I would love to have the chance to ask them. It might be useful for me to offer a couple of practical examples from my own teaching: Some time ago I was asked to teach Road Safety to a class of six-year-olds. Now if I had wanted to avoid drama, I could have set up a simulation exercise whereby the children had the chance to practice road drill, looking right, looking left and then right again before crossing an imaginary road. But as it was drama I wanted to use, I set up a fictitious situation where we (the class and I) invented a five-year-old boy called Michael who on his birthday rushed home from school instead of waiting for his parent and was knocked down by a car. Now we did not simulate the accident. I chose that I should be in role as Michael's parent and the class as Michael's neighbours. And what we experienced was the parent arriving home, thinking Michael must surely have got home first and was hiding; 'Michael? ... Michael, I know you're hiding...' I called, at first in fun and then, as the silence followed each call, more and more desperately ... now including the neighbours to ask whether they had seen him – perhaps he was hiding in their homes ... And then, on the neighbours advice, phoning the school ... but I was too worried to make the phone call, could one of them ... and so on, until we learnt there had been an accident and that Michael was in hospital ... and that he had run across a road without looking first.

Now for me this is working in the art form. What we experience is that moment when a name is called – and there is no answer. The silence is awesome. I believe that it is this silence that takes us, the children and I together, close to what ignoring the road-safety rules can amount to. And it might motivate them to learn the Safety Code.

Now to ask of the lesson, was it education through the arts or education in the arts, is totally absurd. As far as I was concerned we were working in the art form using elements of theatre and we had a firm grasp of the kind of content we were setting out to explore. As a teacher I am observing (1) their understanding of the theme and (2) whether they can extend the theatrical context I have started: to what extent, for instance, are the children able to enjoy the withholding of the news about the accident, so that the tension of not knowing can be fully experienced?; to what extent can they 'pick up' the effectiveness of the counterpoint between the calling and the silence? This is not using drama as method, although the writers of *The Arts in School* perhaps think it is. Is it really the case that they have watched me and others teach and seen what we attempt to do as simulation practice? Is it really the case that they have read my publications and understood from those that what I am recommending is a non-art form of 'drawing diagrams'?

I will give an example from Secondary teaching, again in order to make my point, choosing material that happened to be in someone's syllabus – this time History. The History text book included a kind of 'dramatic' activity that is 'diagram drawing' at its worst. The authors, in their chapter on the American War of Independence, thought it would be a good idea to include something that looked like a play script and have the rift between the people of

New York and the British Government expressed through the mouths of the owner of a coffee house and a well-known customer visiting from London, each character's dialogue stating the opposing arguments in a way that would help the class remember the relevant viewpoints. Now this is an example of simulation, the equivalent of practising Road Safety. The students will no doubt remember the relevant facts as a result of this illustrative dramatic technique. But it is not Drama. I asked my class to become scriptwriters and to turn the text they had in front of them from their History books into 'real' drama. How do you speak to your customers when you are setting up a business? Supposing that customer riles you with his erroneous political views?... and the class began to realise the meaning of sub-text; it is the constraint on the owner of the coffee shop that makes the drama; it is the things that are not said that matter. And the paradox of working in the art form of drama in this way is that, like the silence when Michael does not answer, we are drawn nearer to the meaning of what is going on because it remains implicit. Again, it becomes nonsense to ask whether we are working through the arts or in the arts.

I agree with the writers that we should be clearer in our minds about what we mean by progression in the arts. In one or two recent articles I have been attempting to identify what are the aspects of theatre we want our young children to learn about if they are to get the most out of their classroom drama. A few months ago a reader warned me that if I pursued this, some people would misinterpret what I was doing as recommending teaching for skills at the expense of teaching for content. I pointed out to him that as I had always worked at improving theatre skills in my pupils as we worked towards some new understanding, the fact that I was momentarily concentrating on clarifying what exactly those skills were, could not possibly mislead. Having read *The Arts 5-16*, I suspect that my critic's comments were apt and timely. Consequently in the book I am currently writing, I find myself reiterating 'Although... I may appear to be writing about a theatre skill in this paragraph, I am doing so in the context of drama for understanding the world we live in and ourselves in that world.' Had the writers of *The Arts 5-16* continually referred back to this central objective, then what they have to say about progress becomes relevant. As it stands, it is likely that in answer to the question 'What is the teaching and learning going on in your classrooms today?', a teacher influenced by this new publication is more often than not likely to answer in terms of skills or knowledge about the art.

Of course it is central to *The Arts 5-16* author's thesis that there is a generic framework that can be applied to all arts. While offering a generic framework, they seem unperturbed by the uneven treatment of the arts by the National Curriculum Council. (No 'althoughs' in dealing with government policy either!) Now I can see how it would become very awkward if people claimed that the initial brave statements to do with the arts as modes of under-standing the world should be regarded as main objectives, if music, dance and poetry teachers started to ask understanding what in respect of each thing created, for whereas it is relatively easy to articulate in which ways a group of pupils in drama are, say, 'challenging prevailing attitudes and values', other art forms may not be so amenable to that degree of explicitness. For writers to pursue this further might expose too grave a weakness in their generic idea. So they prefer to treat arts teachers like banana growers and tomato growers who are given the same book of instructions because both parties are concerned with fruit-growing – politically expedient and con-venient no doubt. For what the arts have in common is of central concern to the writers and, indeed, if we were to ignore the basic flaw (as no doubt many people will) then we can only be impressed with the elaboration of theory that follows. From the point of view of drama teachers it represents at least a big improvement on *The Arts in Schools* (1982), which virtually ignored class-room drama – there are no 'althoughs' about that either, indeed that parti-cular publication seems to be treated as unchallengeable 'given'.

I do in fact share the view that there is much in common between the arts and that in so far as they represent what the writers call 'modes of understanding', I recognise that drama uniquely involves all those modes: enactive, visual, aural, kinaesthetic and verbal. For this reason, drama teachers have always found it relatively easy to move from one mode to another. I also agree with the authors' insistence that progress in the ability to 'appraise' an art process and product, especially their own, should be complementary to improve-ment in the 'making' process. As far back as the '60s Dorothy Heathcote em-phasised the importance of reflection on the work done. Again drama's affinity to other arts has often led teachers to use drawing, poetry writing, story-making or dance as a form of reflection.

I also agree with the distinction they draw between artistic and aesthetic; the latter is usefully defined as 'sensitivity to the formal qualities of objects and events'. I have always been interested in identifying the formal elements of theatre and how teacher and pupils can harness these elements in their making of drama. The authors of *The Arts 5-16* are right to urge us to identify them and to find some agreement about what we mean by progress. As I have discussed elsewhere, I believe such elements are to do with focus, tension, manipulation of time and space, constraints and symbolisation. The DES publication, *Drama 5-16* (1989) was a long way from giving attention to these theatrical elements. No doubt the Arts Council's informal drama working group to the National Curriculum Council is at this very moment considering how one might identify achievement in these basic theatre elements, although, if they are also made up of people who look at significant classroom practice and relegate it to 'a method of teaching across the curriculum', and who want to distinguish between education for the arts and education in the arts, then their attempt to offer teachers attainment targets is likely to be misleading and even destructive.

FINALLY

It's all theatre

This article first appeared in *Drama Research*, (2000) Volume 1, April, 21-29. The text in italics was supplied as the introduction to the article and explains its purpose clearly.

The argument of this paper is that whereas the history of drama education has been marked by a concern shared among its pioneers to establish a separate-ness from theatre, now is the time to recognise that all dramatic activities are rooted in theatre. The writer claims that the acknowledgement of such a common basis for practice in the art will lead to a greater tolerance of diversity in an educational context.

The world of music is shared by professionals and children. We say of both groups that they make or play music. But if we replace the word 'music' with the word 'theatre', we are inclined to say that whereas theatre is what actors engage with, what children do isn't to be called theatre. In the past we would do anything to avoid calling it theatre, qualifying the term 'drama' into 'child' drama or 'process' drama or replacing the name of specific classroom practice with non-drama expressions such as 'movement' or 'speech-training'. I once suggested to Peter Slade, somewhat disingenuously, that his classroom practice could have been called 'Child Theatre' instead of 'Child Drama'. I was responding to his own description of classroom dramatic activity at its best: after observing a lesson in school he wrote 'a very clear, exceedingly beautiful piece of theatre is acted out before our eyes...' (Slade, 1954:68). But, having heard my suggestion, he looked at me (justifiably!) with a mixture of astonishment and incredulity that I had failed to grasp the very basis of his mission to demonstrate to people (teachers, parents, doctors and people working in the theatre) that each child has his private world of drama that should be nurtured through education and was distinctly different from theatre. And yet he could not resist identifying some moments of its achieve-ments as 'theatre' – those moments when a class of children reached a peak of artistry in their harmonious use of time and space. If these formal elements for

Slade amounted to 'theatre', why could he not have used that particular label? The answer, of course, lies in his mission to emphasise a particular aspect of dramatic behaviour that he had observed in children. And when you have a mission you need to find a way of drawing attention to something others have not yet seen. And one way of making it quite clear that you are not talking about anything that has gone before is to give it a new name, in this case 'Child Drama'.

I want to argue in this paper that the whole of the 20th century in this country has been taken up with pioneers of new approaches being driven (necessarily driven) to invent new titles in order to stand out from current practice. New labels competed for attention, but their originators all appeared to agree on one thing – whatever was to be done in advancing new practice was not theatre.

I want to suggest that what we have all been doing is indeed theatre and that it is about time we acknowledged it more fully. I propose now to consider in some detail what criteria determine the basis of theatre. Before doing so, let me briefly give a few examples of theatre-avoidance in the past.

Harriet Finlay-Johnson (1911) and Henry Caldwell-Cook (1917) whose pupils engaged straightforwardly in the writing, rehearsing and performing of scripts, coined the term 'dramatisation' and 'playway' respectively. From the 1920s onwards it had to be called 'Speech-training'[1] or it couldn't find a place in schools. 'Mime' (Mawer, 1932) then became the new approved label, outdoing 'Eurhythmics' (Jacques-Dalcroze, 1921). And then came Peter Slade's and Brian Way''s (1967) new conception of a dramatic development derived from natural child play. 'Creative drama' became the in vogue expression that was thought to capture their combined philosophies. Across the Atlantic 'Creative Dramatics' (Ward, 1930) had long been used as an alternative to theatre education. The arrival of Rudolf Laban (1948) in England popularised the idea that drama was really part of physical education. These national influences were followed in the 1960s by the work from Newcastle and Durham Universities which became known as 'Drama in Education', a term that in fact first appeared in print in 1921[2], but in the '60s and '70s became associated with the use of teacher-in-role and whole class 'living through' dramatic activity. Dorothy Heathcote always claimed that she was working in 'theatre', a view I used to find very difficult to swallow, but she never got round to changing the name of her courses to 'teaching teachers to use theatre', because it would certainly have been misunderstood. More recently, 'process drama' has become the fashionable term. Coined by Brad Haseman (1991) and John O'Toole

(1992), it was taken up somewhat reluctantly by Cecily O'Neill when her students in Columbus, Ohio, persuaded her of the need to find a title for her courses that made it clear both to her University and to potential students that the emphasis, far from offering a training in school play production, was that the drama experience itself was to be 'its own destination' (1995). She knew it was vitally important at that stage of the development of drama education in America that her courses' distinctiveness from traditional theatre training should be retained. Most British schools today simply call it 'drama'. If the word 'theatre' appears on the school timetable, it has to be linked with 'Theatre Studies', an unmistakable examination orientation.

We have lived with a century of confusion. I want to suggest that now is the time to call all the activities 'theatre', that delaying doing so perpetuates the past bewilderment and the political factions. Mine is, I hope, more than a pragmatic gesture. I would like to try to offer a conceptual basis for my recommendation. I have to pose two basic questions: 'What is theatre?' and 'To what extent are we justified conceptually in subsuming the wide range of dramatic activities available to children of all ages under this definition?'

How should we define theatre?

A building? Or a social occasion?

If it is to be merely defined as 'what takes place in a building called a theatre', then such a definition, based on its architectural characteristics, would certainly save us the trouble of trying to capture its essence as an artistic activity. It would of course exclude street theatre, Punch and Judy shows, school drama lessons, and drama workshops. On the other hand, if it were broadened out to include any encounter between actors and audience, as Ken Robinson (1980) argued, then that would be to emphasise the social aspect of the art: there must be actors; and there must be an audience for them to play to. The occasion and the interaction become the defining characteristics. This seems an utterly reasonable definition of theatre, but one that again fails to tell us about the activity itself.

Can theatre be defined by the 'content' of the drama?

Definitions depend on where you are standing! Let us, while accepting that an important feature of theatre is indeed the occasion of actors sharing something with an audience, leave Ken Robinson's 'social encounter' for the moment and take a different angle. Suppose we tried to define theatre by its content. Most plays are about telling lies, or at least about withholding or not knowing or not facing the truth. In these terms theatre is always about unfolding some truth and is dependent on one or more of the characters or the audience having the wrong or insufficient information. Kenneth Tynan in the '50s in putting it more elegantly broadened it to embrace the necessary suffering of one or more of the characters. For him theatre includes: 'an ordered sequence of events that brings one or more of the people into a desperate condition which it must always explain and should, if possible, resolve' (1957). This definition seems to say what theatre is all about and it comes close to what guided me in structuring my own classroom practice from the mid '60s onwards – we used to call it 'A Man in a Mess'. As a drama teacher I recognised this parallel with theatre but would not have dreamed of calling it 'theatre' – because I was caught up in the idea that drama in education must be private. I would try to set up all sorts of 'desperation' sequences for my classes (I shudder when I recall some of the risks I took!) so that they could think about their experience and learn from it. Such a 'content' for drama lessons did indeed coincide with theatre practice. Both involved a resolution of social, psychological or cataclysmic situations. Dorothy in her very early days (model number one) (2000) often reflected these different levels of suffering by beginning a lesson with: 'Do you want our play to be about big'uns telling littl'uns what to do; or people trying to get on with each other but finding their differences get in the way; or do you want us to be people having to put up with something from outside that they can't control?' It is worth noting Dorothy's phrasing here, for the popular notion in Drama workshops at the time was that the content of theatre was conflict. She avoided saying 'big'uns against littl'uns'. She did not want her classes automatically to fall in with the shouting matches that at that time characterised dramatic improvisations throughout secondary and adult drama training.

Narrative appears to be significant but not critical
While Dorothy moved away from this model towards Mantle of the Expert, it took me a long time to realise that what I was doing in the classroom was structurally limiting, that there was more to drama than dealing with perpetual crisis. For instance, I gradually accepted the use of 'depiction'. I learnt that there is such a thing as a 'moment of theatre', for example, a depiction by a small group representing, say, a photograph or a still moment of action, perhaps accompanied by voice-overs expressing personal thoughts or underlying implications. This simultaneous exposure of many levels of meaning was just as illuminating, indeed in practice often more profound, because it is sometimes easier for youngsters to handle than a structured 'living through' experience leading to a crisis. Like Peter Slade, but in a quite different context, I was saying, 'Eureka! This is theatre!'.

Back to audience rather than content – introducing 'self-spectatorship'

But if this is theatre, and if what Slade recognised when his classes filled the space with harmonious shapes and sounds is theatre, then we can no longer cling to Kenneth Tynan's necessary sequence of desperate events for our definition. One can only agree that although most theatre may rely on such a narrative, it may not be its defining feature. So are we brought back to the presence of an audience as the basic characteristic? Certainly, a rigorously prepared depiction absolutely relies on an audience. And this is where we have to accept the idea of 'self-spectatorship'. When we make anything we are spectators to it. A four-year old drawing her mother is a spectator to her own drawing. That same child 'playing at being mother' is an audience to what is being created. And so in school drama. Even in Slade's work, when there is no conventional audience present, 'teacher's expectations of us' sharpens the self-monitoring, a self-spectatorship that provides an incipient 'audience'. His classes are watching what they are creating as they create it. If what they achieve is arresting, harmonious, or meaningful, they must apprehend this achievement. Any creative act needs someone to know that it is creative – and that there is an 'it' that has been created.

The introduction of 'self-spectatorship' as a dimension of 'audience' is critical to my argument. The possibility of your accepting my recommendation that all forms of dramatic activity potentially qualify as 'theatre' is dependent on your also accepting 'self-spectatorship' as a necessary component. The special 'attention' of the audience to what is going on becomes part of the equation. Can we describe the nature of that attention?

What is the audience actively doing? – 'reading into an action or object and treating it as fiction'

This I believe provides the key to defining theatre. Thus not only must the audience (including the 'spectator' component of the players) see what is going on as something created, they must further see it 'as meaningful in a fictional context', that is, going beyond the immediate sense of the action by pointing to something beyond itself. A football match, in these terms, cannot be theatre, for the spectators' attention is drawn to the event itself and therein satisfyingly lies its significance. But a football match played on stage takes on what Bruce Wilshire (1982:xi-xii) calls 'an incarnated universal'. Without sacrificing its particularity it 'stands for' football matches and their related themes of competition, opposing sides, rivalry, sportsmanship, rules or whatever the dramatist wants it to point to. The meaning lies both in the particular

167

and in its generalisations and the audience treats it as fiction, both enjoying what is happening and looking for the implications of what is happening. They ask themselves 'What is the significance of what is going on here?'

Thus theatre takes place when spectators choose to 'read into' an event or an object and treat it as fiction. When the curtain goes up to reveal a single empty chair on a stage the audience start 'reading into' it and treating it as fiction. This is theatre. But if we shift from conventional theatre to what goes on in schools, that use of the empty chair does not change. An empty chair placed in a space at the front of a classroom is an invitation to the rest of the class to start 'reading into' it. When the teacher (in role) points silently to the empty chair she has placed at the other end of the hall, all the children start 'reading into' it. And I will go as far as to suggest (this will be returned to later) that when a child in solitary play places a chair in a certain way on a certain spot s/he is 'reading into' it.

Space and time are 'freed'

In each of these contexts the empty chair becomes a fictional chair in a fictional place in a fictional time. Both space and time are now freed for manipulation. The staged football match or the staged wedding becomes foreshortened, mere fictional indications of events, not the real events. Exceptionally, time and space coincide with real time and space. For instance, suppose, as part of a drama on stage or in the classroom, a character was required to give an exhibition of juggling. This kind of activity can only be done 'for real', using 'real' time and space, but within the overall context of what went before and what could follow its fictional status is sustained; the spectators continue to see it as theatre while at the same time appreciating the very real accomplishment of the performer. But supposing the character juggling went on and on ... and on. Would there not come a point when whatever the fiction was supposed to be could hardly be sustained, when the event ceases to be theatre and becomes entertaining only in itself and for itself? The initial fiction would now only be there as a point of reference in people's minds awaiting resumption.

Introducing the notion in an educational context of theatre 'awaiting resumption'

This is what happens in Dorothy Heathcote's Mantle of the Expert work. When Dorothy puts up a notice saying 'Manager's Office; Please come in', she is inviting her class to work in theatre; when she announces 'The mail's arrived – this one looks sort of important ...shall I?' she is working in theatre.

When she says 'One of the designers here (indicating a member of the class) would like a word with you all ... she has an idea ...', she is inviting the adolescent as 'the designer' to work in theatre. But then there are long periods when the class are actually drawing a design or actually drafting reports or actually looking something up in the library, when the reality of real time and space has taken over, when theatre virtually disappears. Virtually, not entirely, for it remains as a point of reference in people's minds 'awaiting resumption'. Most of the time in Mantle of the Expert, therefore, the fiction will not be to the fore. This may seem less strange when we consider that even in a typical Theatre Studies class a great deal of time can be given over to non-theatre activities such as discussion, studying a text, researching a character or a social history, learning about theatre history, the practising of movement or voice skills or painting a set – during which theatre is there as a 'point of reference', awaiting resumption.

There will be resistance

I am claiming that all children's dramatic activities are concerned with 'reading into' the particular and treating it as fiction, that all are theatre. Such a claim will cause unease in many quarters, among whom, of course, will be people who work in 'the theatre'. It requires such people to accept that some school dramatic activities that appear to have little in common with conventional theatre should be regarded as additional theatrical genres, because they all share this capacity for 'reading into' and making fiction out of a perceived action or object.

Perhaps the greatest unease will be felt by those for whom Process Drama or Drama in Education is indeed 'its own destination', or by those who work in drama therapy, cherishing the uniqueness of children's creativity as a natural extension of child play. As I said at the beginning of this address, many pioneers have devoted their careers to demonstrating the value of something very special and precious rooted in the natural imagination and creativity of the young child. I want to suggest that what a young child is about is indeed 'making theatre'. I've not come across anyone putting this forward precisely in these terms, but it seems to me that if theatre is definable as 'a spectator reading into the particular and treating it as fiction' then this is what most young children are doing when they play.

An argument for seeing children's dramatic play as theatre

The Russian psychologist, Lev Vygotsky (1933) gave us a theoretical underpinning of play activity that points us in the direction I am now taking. He saw the overriding outcome of child play as reducing the status of action in favour of meaning. As he put it: 'Action retreats to second place and becomes the pivot' for meaning. This is exactly what happens in theatre. The empty chair becomes a pivot for 'the making of fictional meaning'; the few moments of juggling become a pivot for 'reading in' new meanings. What a pity play theorists of Vygotsky's time and since failed to call it theatre. If only, instead of saying 'When a child plays', they had said 'When a child makes theatre ...' just as they had no difficulty with saying 'When a child draws ...'

What is sought by the spectator is an underlying structure of values, beliefs, rules etc.

To conclude, then, I have tried to argue that all forms of make-believe qualify for theatre, if there is a spectator reading into the object or action for fictional meaning. That spectator may be no more than the spectator in oneself or it may be the audience in a conventional theatre. It is important to note that this definition has become two dimensional. 'Looking into the object or action for meaning' combines both a 'mental intention' on the part of the audience and a kind of 'content' within the drama. If we recall Wilshire's definition quoted above, he writes of an 'incarnated universal' as that content. I think 'universal' may be misleading, for it would be inappropriate to claim that there are universal 'truths' to be searched for by the spectator. I believe what is searched for is a 'structure', the underlying dynamic governing an action or the placing of an object. The spectator asks, to use a phrase of David Best, 'What does the empty chair amount to?' (1985). What are the possible underlying values or rules or parameters or laws?

Summarising definitional preferences

To summarise, in the Western world 'going to the theatre' is an exclusive life-style that may adequately define theatre for the privileged – a place to visit. For many it is a unique kind of sharing between audience and performers – theatre is an interaction between actors and audience. For others its narrative content of a crisis resolved is central. I have argued that its content is indeed part of its defining characteristic, but it is its hidden, structural content that can only be discovered if there is someone asking 'What might be the values, causes, parameters, rules or laws here in this particular fictional context?' This, I believe, is what often happens when a child plays at 'being mother'. The very phrase that I used above 'playing at being mother' takes us in the wrong direction, for when s/he plays s/he is not pretending to be mother, but rather, s/he is posing the more generalising question of 'What are the rules here – in my 'mother's context?' – and this is theatre in the broad sense I am advocating.

170

So, what should be done?

It is all theatre, but for anyone to recommend an immediate change of usage would be absurd, for there are too many branches of education that still rely on alternative expressions to make it clear to others that what they are doing is something other than or bigger than putting on plays. For example, the most recently created professorship in our field by the University of Central England, has been given the specific title 'professor of drama in education'[3] and the students taking that institution's MA courses specifically graduate as MA in Drama in Education. Students applying from all over the world need to know that the courses on offer will prepare them to work in education. I notice, however, that Griffiths University staff in Brisbane are now calling their courses 'Applied Theatre'. I respond warmly to this innovation, while recognising it cannot suit everyone.

But I am trying to appeal for something more important than changing a name. I am suggesting that in this coming century we re-educate practitioners to think theatre. If everyone knows that everything they make is theatre then the term may indeed appear more often in titles, but more important than that is the desirability that all teachers recognise they are sharing the same common ground. All drama courses, all drama activities, will be seen as practising one or more theatrical genres. All attempts to weave new theories will have the basic principles of theatre as their shared point of departure. We can then acknowledge, respect, enjoy and understand important differences in emphasis and practice.

Those differences must be sustained and new ones allowed to flourish. I am not advocating a narrow practice of training in and studying of conventional theatre, as I know some blinkered leaders would have it. I am appealing for the opposite. I am inviting a more generous view of different practices based on sound educational principles and a vision of what education ought to be. We need to stop imagining that we are looking across a gulf separating those who work in theatre and those who do something less than theatre. We are all working in theatre and the question we have to ask at every stage in the educational system is which theatre *genre* will be the most appropriate for this particular age group, or for this particular social grouping, or in respect of this particular image of the best kind of education? Whether one form of practice is superior to another should no longer depend, as it seems to in some quarters, on how close it comes to conventional training, but on the quality of the learning experience. My paper is an appeal for a breadth of vision from teachers who, because they are secure in the knowledge that they share the same fundamental basis for their work, can feel free to branch out and experiment. Such teachers have a right, if they wish, to call their own form of theatre practice by its own special name. Acknowledging the same theatrical root allows for a greater tolerance of diversity.[4]

Notes

1 See. for instance, *Teaching of English in England* (1921) HMSO

2 *ibid*

3 I am referring to David Davis, Department of Education, University of Central England

4 Should any reader care to respond to the above text, my e-mail address is: gavbol@waitrose.com

Afterword

Dear Reader

The classroom, school hall or studio you are working in now, I entered some 60 years ago, dabbling in what I thought school drama was all about – rehearsing plays, speech training and confidence building. But about every five years the fashion changed and I had to catch up. I wonder which fashionable *genre* you are caught up with in 2010? Whatever the current vogue, no doubt the one aspect we share is the excitement and belief in what we are doing while, paradoxically, never being quite sure of the outcome of a particular project! This is drama teaching, living on the edge of the art form we love.

My career landed me with the chance to formulate some kind of theoretical background to classroom practice, identifying principles that became modified as fashions changed and as we all became more critically aware of gaps in our understanding of what we were doing, or as Cecily O'Neill, in her perceptive Foreword to this Collection puts it: ...revisiting 'ideas in the light of fresh insights of his own or other theorists...'. I was usefully challenged by practitioners who offered alternative views and arguments. Indeed rethinking our aims and priorities is essential to development in our subject. But it sometimes happens that in our determination to re-shape our practice we are unwittingly, or even deliberately, casting aside ways of thinking that could perhaps still be of value today.

I am very grateful to Professor Davis for taking the trouble to collect my past writings and select those for this book. You may find that, here and there, there are theoretical arguments put forward that could reopen some doors on practice today. Or the opposite may happen: that reading about my ways of looking at classroom drama may simply, but equally usefully, reinforce and even sharpen the value of your current ideals. Either way, 2010 should be seen as part of an evolving, development process, for we still have a long way to go in understanding the rich potential of drama education.

With regards
Gavin Bolton
Reader [very] Emeritus, University of Durham
May 2010

References

Allen, J (1979) *Drama in Schools: its theory and practice*. London: Heinemann

Bateson, G (1976) A theory of play and fantasy. In Bruner, J S *et al* (1976) *Play: its development and evolution*, Penguin

Bentley, E (ed) (1968) *The Theory of Modern Stage: An Introduction to Modern Theatre*, New York: Pelican

Bentley, E (1975) *The Life of Drama*, New York: Atheneum

Best, D (1985) *Feeling and Reason in the Arts*, London: Allen and Unwin

Best, D (1992) *The Rationality of Feeling*, London, Falmer

Boal, A (1981) Theatre de Popprime, Numero 5. *Creditade*: An 03.

Bolton, G (1971) Drama and theatre in education: a survey. In *Drama and theatre in education*. Dodd, N and Hickson, W (Eds) London:Heinemann

Bolton, G (1972) Further notes for Bristol teachers on the 'second dimension'. In Gavin *Bolton: selected writings* (1986) London and New York: Longman

Bolton G (1978) Emotion in the dramatic process – Is it an adjective or verb? *National Association for Drama in Education Journal* (Australia). 3 (Dec.): pp 14-18.

Bolton, G (1979) *Towards a theory of drama in education*. London: Longman

Bolton, G (1984) *Drama as education: an argument for placing drama at the centre of the curriculum*. Harlow: Longman

Bolton, G (1989) Drama. In Hargreaves, D (ed) *Children and the arts*. Milton Keynes: Open University Press

Bolton, G (1990) *Four aims in drama teaching*. London Drama London Drama Association

Bolton, G (1992) *New perspectives on classroom drama*. Simon and Schuster Education

Bolton, G (1998) *Acting in classroom drama: a critical analysis*. Trentham Books

Bolton, G (2010) *Personal email*

Brecht, B (1949) A new technique of acting. In T*heatre Arts*, 33 no. 1 Jan.

Brook, P (1968) T*he Empty Space*, New York: Atheneum

Brook, P (1993) *There are no secrets*, London: Methuen

Bruner, J (1971) *The relevance of education*. New York: Norton

Bullough, E (1912) Psychical distance as a factor in art and as an aesthetic principle. *British Journal of Psychology*, 5, part 2: 87-118

Burton, E.J. (1949) *Teaching English through Self-Expression: A Course in Speech, Mime and Drama*. London: Evans

Caloustie Gulbenkian Foundation (1982) *The arts in schools*. London: Caloustie

Carroll, J (1980) *The Treatment of Dr. Lister.* Mitchell College of Advanced Education, Bathurst Australia

Cassirer, E (1953) *The Philosophy of Symbolic Forms* translated by R. Manhheim, New Haven: Yale University Press

Cook, C. H (1917) *The Play Way: An Essay in Educational Method,* London: Heinemann,

Courtney, R (1968) *Play, drama and thought.* Simon and Pierre

Davis, D (1976) What is Depth in Educational Drama? in *Young Drama* Vol 4 No 3 October

Department of Education and Science (1984) *English from 5 to 16: Curriculum Matters 1.* London: H.M.S.O.

Department of Education and Science (1989) *Drama from 5 to 16: Curriculum Matters 17* HMSO, London

Department of Education and Science (1990) *The teaching and learning of drama (aspects of primary education)* London: HMSO

Eisner, E (1974) Examining some myths in art education. *Student Art Education*, 15 (3): 7-16.

Fines, J and Verrier, R (1974) *The drama of history.* New University Education

Finlay-Johnson, H (1911) *The Dramatic Method of Teaching*, Nisbet Self-Help Series, James Nisbet, London

Fleming, M (1982) A philosophical investigation into drama in education. PhD thesis, University of Durham.

Fleming, M (1994) *Starting Drama Teaching,* Fulton London

Fleming, M (1997) *The Art of Drama Teaching*, London: Fulton

Fleming, M (2001) *Teaching drama in primary and secondary schools: an integrated approach*, David Fulton Publishers

Frost, A and Yarrow R (1990) *Improvisation in Drama*, Macmillan, Basingstoke

Gillham, G (1974) Condercum school report for Newcastle upon Tyne LEA (unpublished)

Hall, E.T. (1959, 1981) *The Silent Language.* London: Anchor Books, Doubleday

Harré, R (1983), An analysis of social activity: a dialogue with Rom Harré. In States of mind: conversations with psychological investigators, Miller, J (Ed) BBC London

Haseman, B (1991) *The Drama Magazine: The Journal of National Drama*, July, pp19-21

Heathcote, D (2000) Contexts for active learning: four models to forge links between schooling and society, in: *Drama Research*, Lawrence (ed.), London: National Drama

Heathcote, D and Bolton, G (1995) *Drama for Learning: Dorothy Heathcote's Mantle of the Expert Approach to Education*, New Hampshire: Heinemann

Holmes, E (1911) *What is and what might be.* London: Constable

Hornbrook, D (1989) *Education and Dramatic Art.* Oxford: Blackwell

Hornbrook, D (1998) *Education and Dramatic Art (2nd Ed.)* Oxford: Blackwell

Hourd, M. L. (1949) *The Education of the Poetic Spirit: A Study in Children's Expression in the English Language*, London: Heinemann

Isaacs, S (1933) *Social Development of Young Children*, Routledge and Keegan Paul, London

Jacques-Dalcroze, E (1921) *Rhythm and Music in Education* trans. by Harold F. Rubenstein, London: Chatto and Windus

Johnstone, K. (1981) *Impro: improvisation and theatre.* London: Methuen

Kempe, A. (1990) *The GCSE drama coursebook.* Oxford: Blackwell Education

REFERENCES

Kleberg, L (1993, trans by Charles Rougle) *Theatre as Action*, London: Macmillan

Laban, R (1948) *Modern Educational Dance*, London: Macdonald and Evans

Langdon, E.M. (1949) *An Introduction to Dramatic Work with Children*, London: Dennis Dobson

Luria, AR and Yudovich, FY (1959) *Speech and the development of mental processes in the child.* Staples Press

Mackenzie, F (1935) *The Amateur Actor*, London: Nelson

Maslow, A. (1954) *Motivation and personality.* New York: Harper

Mather, R (1996) Turning Drama Conventions into Images. In *Drama* Vol 4 No 3/Vol 5 No 1 The Journal of National Drama

Mawer, I (1932) *The Art of Mime,* London: Methuen

McGregor, L *et al* (1977) *The Schools Council Drama Teaching Project (10-16)*, London; Heinemann

McGregor, L, Tate, M, Robinson, K (1977) *Learning through drama, Schools Council Drama Teaching Project (10-16).* Heinemann.

Millward, P (1988) The Language of Drama Vols 1 and 2, unpublished Ph.D thesis, University of Durham

Morgan, N. and Saxton, J. (1991) *Teaching, Questioning and Learning.* London: Routledge and Kegan Paul

National Curriculum Council (1990) *The Arts 5-16.* York: Oliver and Boyd

Nelson, K and Seidman, S (1984) in *Symbolic Play* by Inge Bretherton (ed) London: Academic Press

Newton, R. G (1937) *Acting Improvised*, London: Nelson

O'Neil, C (1995) Drama Worlds: A framework for Process. *Drama*, pxi, Portsmouth, NH: Heinemann

O'Toole, J (1992) *The Process of Drama: Negotiating Art and Meaning,* London: Routledge

Perls, F (1969) *Gestalt therapy.* Moab: Verbatim Real People Press

Piaget, J (1972) *Play, dreams and imitation in childhood.* London: Routledge and Kegan Paul

Plowden Report (1967) *Children and their primary schools.* HMSO.

Polanyi, M. (1958) *Personal Knowledge: towards a post-critical philosophy.* London: Routledge and Kegan Paul

Reid, A L (1982) The concept of aesthetic education. In Ross M (ed) *The development of aesthetic experience.*

Robinson, K [ed] (1980) *Exploring Theatre and Education*, London: Heinemann

Robinson, K (1981) A re-evaluation of the roles and functions of drama in secondary education with reference to a survey of curricular drama in 259 secondary schools. PhD thesis, University of London.

Rogers, C. (1961) *On becoming a person.* Boston: Houghton-Mifflin

Ross, M (1978) *The creative arts.* Heinemann.

Ross, M (1982) The development of aesthetic experience. *Curriculum series in the arts* Vol 3, Pergammon Press

Schechner, R (1977) *Performance Theory*, London: Routledge

Schechner, R (1982) *The End of Humanism Performing Arts*, New York: Journal Publications

Schiller, F (1965) *On the aesthetic education of man* (trans R Snell). Frederick Ungar, New York. (First published 1795.)

Slade, P (1954) *Child drama*. University of London Press.

Smith, L and Schumacher, S (1977) Extended pilot trials of the Aesthetics Education Program: a qualitative description, analysis and evaluation. In Hamilton D *et al.* (eds) *Beyond the numbers game*. Macmillan, pp. 314-30.

States, B (1985) *Great Reckonings in Little Rooms,* Los Angeles: University of Californian Press

Stone, R.L. (1949) *The Story of a School*, HMSO

Sully, J (1896) *Studies of Childhood,* London: Longman Green

Tormey, A (1971) *The concept of expression.* Princeton University Press.

Tynan, K (1957) *Declarations*, MacGibbon and Kee

Vygotsky, L (1933 orig; trans. 1976) Play and its role in the mental development of the child, in: *Play*, by Bruner, J. *et al*, p550, Harmondsworth: Penguin Education

Vygotsky, L (1978) *Mind in society, the development of higher psychological processes.* London: Harvard University Press

Ward, W (1930) *Creative Dramatics*, New York: Appleton

Way, B (1967) Development through drama London; Longman

Wilshire, B (1982) *Role-Playing and Identity: The Limits of Theatre Metaphor,* Bloomington: Indiana University Press

Witkin, R W (1974) *The intelligence of feeling.* London: Heinemann Educational books

Gavin Bolton, an incomplete bibliography for future researchers, in place of an archive

Towards a Theory of Drama in Education, Longman, London, 1979.

Drama as Education: an argument for placing drama at the centre of the curriculum, Longman, London, 1984.

Selected Writings of Gavin Bolton, (Eds.: D. Davis and C. Lawrence), London, 1986.

New Perspectives on Classroom Drama, Simon and Shuster, London, 1992.

Drama for Learning: Dorothy Heathcote's 'Mantle of the Expert' approach to education (co-author with Heathcote, D) Heinemann, N.J. 1995

Acting in classroom drama: a critical analysis, Trentham, 1998

So you want to use role-play? (co-author with Heathcote, D) Trentham, 1999

Drama för lärande och insikt (a volume of selected writings) A. Grünbaum, (Ed.) Göteborg, Daidalos, 2008

Chapters contributed to books

Drama and Theatre in Education – a Survey, in *Drama and Theatre in Education*, M. Dodd and W. Hickson (Eds.), Heinemann, London, 1971.

Theatre Form in Drama as Process, in *Exploring Theatre and Education*, K. Robinson (Ed.), Heinemann, London, 1980, pp 71-87.

Drama in Education and Theatre in Education – a comparison, in *Theatre in Education: A Casebook*, A.R. Jackson (Ed.), Manchester University Press, 1980, pp49-77.

Drama and Education – a Reappraisal, in *Children and Drama,* N. McCaslin (Ed.), 2nd Edition, Longman, New York, 1981, pp178-191.

An outline of the contemporary view of drama in education in Great Britain, in *Opvoedkundig Drama*, M. Goethals (Ed.), University of Leuven Press, Volume 2, 1981, pp467-475.

Drama and the Curriculum – a philosophical perspective, in *Drama and the Whole Curriculum*, J. Nixon (Ed.), Hutchinson, London, 1982, pp 27-42.

Drama as Learning, As Art and as Aesthetic Experience, in *Development of Aesthetic Experience*, M. Ross (Ed.), Pergamon Press, Oxford, 1982, pp137-147.

Drama in Education: Learning Medium or Arts Process? in *Bolton at the Barbican*, NATD with Longman Group, 1983, pp5-18.

An interview with Gavin Bolton, in *Handbook of Educational Drama and Theatre*, R. Landy (Ed.), New York University Press, 1983, pp43-6.

The activity of dramatic playing, in *Issues in Educational Drama*, C. Day and J, Norman (Eds.), Falmer Press 1983, pp49-63.

Drama – pedagogy or art? in *Dramapaedagogik – i nordisk perspectiv*, J. Szatkowski (Ed.), Artikelsamling, Teaterforlaget, 1985, pp 79-100.

Drama in *Children and the Arts*, D.J. Hargreaves (Ed.), Open University, Milton Keynes and Philadelphia, 1989, pp119-137.

Lernen Durch und uber drama im schulischen Unterricht, in *Drama und Theater in der Schule und fur die Schule*, M. Schewe (Ed.), Universitat Oldenburg, 1990, pp18-24.

The drama education scene in England, Preface to *A Tribute to Catherine Hollingsworth* A. Nicol, 1991 pp4-6

A Brief History of Classroom Drama in *Towards Drama as a Method in the Foreign Language Classroom*, M. Schewe, and P. Shaw, (Eds.) Peter Lang 1993 Frankfurt pp25-42

Una breve storia del classroom drama nella acuola inglese. Una storia di contraddizioni in *Teatro Ed Educazione in Europa: Inghilterra E Belgio*, B. Cuminetti, (Ed.) Guerini Studio, Milano pp45-56.

DRAMA/Drama and Cultural values in *IDEA 95 Papers: Selected Readings in Drama and Theatre Education* (Eds: P. Taylor and C. Hoepper) Nadie Publications 1995 Brisbane, pp. 29-34.

Afterword: Drama as Research in Researching Drama and Arts Education (Ed: P. Taylor) Falmer Press London 1996 pp 187-194

A history of drama education: a search for substance in International handbook of research in arts education, (L. Bresler, Ed) Springer, 2007 pp 45-61

Improvised drama in schools: a history of confusion in *'Talkin' 'bout my generation': archäologie der theaterpadägogik 2* (M Streisand *et al*, Eds) Berlin, Milow, Strasbourg: Schibri-Verlag, 2007 pp54-60

Pamphlet: Gavin Bolton – four articles 1970-1980, NADECT (National Association of teachers of Drama in Education and Children's Theatre), 1980.

Articles in journals

Drama in the Primary School – Support from Local Authorities, in *TES,* No. 2544, 21st February, 1964, p. 428.

The Nature of Children's Drama, in *Education for Teaching,* November, 1966, pp.46-54.

In Search of Aims and Objectives, in *Creative Drama*, Vol. 4, No. 2, Spring 1969 and in Canadian Child Drama Association Journal, April, 1976, pp.5-8.

Drama in Education, in Speech and Drama, Vol. 18, No. 3. Autumn, 1969 pp.10-13.

Is Theatre in Education Drama in Education? in *Outlook,* Journal of the British Children's Theatre Association, Vol. 5, 1973, pp.7-8.

Moral Responsibility in Children's Theatre, in *Outlook,* Journal of the British Children's Theatre Association, Vol. 5, 1973, pp.6-8.

Emotion and Meaning in Creative Drama, in *Canadian Child Drama Association Journal,* February 1976, pp.13-19.

Drama as Metaphor in *Young Drama,* Vol. 4, No. 3, June 1976, pp 43-47. Also in Dokumentatie en Orientate uber de Expressie, (Holland) Dec.76.

Drama Teaching – a Personal Statement, in *Insight*, Journal of the British Children's Theatre Association, Summer 1976, pp.10-12.

Creative Drama and Learning, in *American theatre Association's Children's theatre Review,* February 1977, pp 10-12.

Drama and Emotion – some Uses and Abuses, in *Young Drama*, Vol. 5, No. 1, February 1977, pp 3-12.

Psychical Distancing in Acting, in *The British Journal of Aesthetics,* Vol. 17, No 1, Winter 1977, pp.63-67.

Emotional Effects in Drama, in *Queensland Association of Drama in Education,* Vol. 1, No. 1, October 1976, pp.3-11.

Creative Drama as an Art Form, in *London Drama,* Journal of the London Drama Teachers Association, April 1977, pp.2-9.

Symbolisation in the Process of Improvised Drama, in *Young Drama,* Vol. 6, No 1. 1978, pp.10-13.

The relationship between Drama and Theatre, in *London Drama,* Vol. 5, No. 1, 1978, pp.5-7.

The concept of 'Showing' in Children's Dramatic Activity, in *Young Drama,* Vol. 6, No. 3, October 1978, pp.97-101.

Some Issues Involved in the use of Role-Play with Psychiatric Adult Patients, in *Dramatherapy,* Vol. 2, No 4, June 1979, pp 11-13.

Emotions in the Dramatic Process – is it an Adjective or a Verb?, in *National Association for Drama in Educational Journal,* (Australia), Vol. 3, December, 1978, pp.14-18.

An Evaluation of the Schools Council Drama Teaching (Secondary) Project, in *Speech and Drama,* Vol. 28, No 3, Autumn 1979, pp.14-22.

The Aims of Educational Drama, in *National Association of Drama in Education Journal,* (Australia), Vol. 4, December 1979, pp.28-32.

Imagery in Drama in Education, in *SCYPT Journal* (Standing Conference of Young People's Theatre), No 5, May 1980, pp 5-8.

Assessment of Practical Drama, in *Drama Contact,* Vol. 1, No 4, May, 1980, pp.14-16. (Canada)

Drama as Concrete Action, in *London Drama,* Vol. 6, No. 4, Spring 1981, pp.16-18.

Drama in the Curriculum, in *Drama and Dance,* Vol 1, No 1, Autumn 1981, pp.9- 16.

Teacher-in-role and the learning process, in *SCYPT Journal,* No. 12. 1984, pp.21-26.

Gavin Bolton interviewed by David Davis, in *Drama and Dance,* Vol. 4, Spring 1985, pp.4-14.

Drama and Anti-Racist teaching – a reply to Jon Nixon, in *Curriculum,* Vol. 6, No. 3, Autumn 1985, pp.13-14.

Changes in thinking about Drama in Education, in *Theory into Practice,* Vol XXIV, No. 3, 1985, pp 151-7. (U.S.A.)

Weaving theories is not enough, in *New Theatre Quarterly* (NTQ)), Vol. 11, No. 8, November 1986, pp.369-371.

Off-target, in *London Drama,* Vol. 7, No 4, 1987, pp.22-23.

Drama as Art, in *Drama Broadsheet,* Vol. 5, Issue 3, Autumn, 1988, pp.13-18.

Towards a theory of Dramatic Art – a Personal Statement, in *Drama Broadsheet,* Spring 1990, Vol. 7 Issue 1, pp.2-5.

Although, in *Drama Broadsheet,* Winter 1990, Vol. 7, Issue 3, pp.8-11.

Four aims in *Teaching Drama,* in London Drama, July, 1990

The Changing Room, in *SCYPT Journal,* Spring 1992, No. 23 pp.25-32.

Aristotle and the Art of the Actor in *Drama Contact* (Ontario), No. 15 Autumn 1991

Piss on his Face, in *Broadsheet,* Issue 2, 1992, NATD pp.4-9

Have a Heart!, in *Drama* Vol 1 No 1 Summer 1992 pp.7-8

A Balancing Act, in *The NADIE Journal,* Australia Vol 16 No 4 Winter 1992 pp 16-17

Index

Also from Trentham

EDWARD BOND AND THE DRAMATIC CHILD
Edward Bond's plays for young people
edited by David Davis

This is the first book in English fully to explain Edward Bond's new form of theatre.

Our future depends on the state of our imaginations, and drama becomes more important as the world changes. Plays young people write, act in and watch are the blueprints of the world they will have to live in. Edward Bond argues that drama helps children 'to know themselves and their world and their relation to it' but that neither Brecht nor Stanislavsky can provide a basis for modern theatre.

Edward Bond and the Dramatic Child discusses all Bond's important plays for young people and offers case studies of various productions of them. Contributors explore the demands and rewards of a cting and staging Bond.

The book will be of interest to everyone working in drama with young people in theatre, schools or community work, and to actors and directors in mainstream theatre.

The contributors are Edward Bond, David Allen, Chris Cooper, Tony Coult, John Doona, Kate Katafiasz, Bill Roper and David Davis. The glossary explains Bond's theatre terminology.

Professor David Davis is founder of The International Centre for Studies in Drama in Education, at the University of Central England.

2005, ISBN 978 1 85856 312 1
244 pages, 247 x 168mm, £20.99

www.trentham-books.co.uk